DIRTY OLD RAGS

DIRTY OLD RAGS

LORI RUSH

XULON PRESS

Xulon Press
2301 Lucien Way #415
Maitland, FL 32751
407.339.4217
www.xulonpress.com

Scripture quotations taken from the Holy Bible, New International
Version®, NIV® Copyright ©1973, 1978, 1984, 2011 by Biblica, Inc.®
Used by permission. All rights reserved worldwide..

Printed in the United States of America.

ISBN-13: 978-1-54566-893-1

Table of Contents

Acknowledgments

Momma, thank you for teaching me who Christ is. I love you now to eternity. Kenny, Kasey, Kyle, and Lindsey, I thank God for you every day. We could not have imagined what God had in store for us. I'm so glad you're mine.

Introduction

Two years ago, God spoke to me in a dream. He said, "You are going to write a book, and it will be titled, 'Dirty Old Rags.'" I saw an outline of this book in my dream, and as various scenes from my life appeared before my eyes, I heard God's voice say, "It will take two years to complete."

That was 2016. I have learned that when God speaks, listen!

I believe He wants us to know He finds value in each one of us regardless of our past, age, status, or circumstance. He can use every part of our imperfect lives to grow the kingdom. Only God knows the purpose He created us for. If we are not afraid to follow, He will show us!

God is still in the business of miracles. He's doing them for people like us every day. This is my imperfect miraculous journey that has led me to see beauty in trials along the way.

Dedication

I pray whoever is the intended receiver of this writing picks it up and has the prowess to hear the message inside: May they know that in our own strength, we are merely "Dirty Old Rags." It is only through the Blood of Christ that we can be made clean. Only through Christ may we have eternal life. Great things can be accomplished in His name and for His glory with imperfect people like us.

I believe now is a time for harvest and He is working with those that are willing.

Endorsements

I have just finished reading "Dirty Old Rags" and I am excited to not only endorse but I would recommend it to everyone to read this. I know Lori and her family. I have been her Pastor but most of all her friend. I appreciate how open and honest she is in the book but understand if you have ever met her reading the book is just like a conversation. This story is so real and relevant. A message of Grace, Mercy, Love and Redemption. Showing that no matter what, God has a plan. Never give up and never give in. When you are at your weakest, God shows up in a big way. Thank you, Lori for these beautiful words of encouragement and when I get "home" I'll see you at the East Gate!

Pastor Mike Seay
Former First Baptist Church Minco Pastor

I have read many books, or I should say read parts of many books. When I started reading "Dirty Old Rags" there was simply no place to stop. Once you read this book there can be no possible way of denying the power and love of our Lord Jesus Christ.

From page to page I could feel the presence and love of the Lord. It is hard to read with tear filled eyes, but I could sense the will of the Lord being fulfilled. Coincidences are something people talk about; everything that happens is part of God's plan. For several years now we have seen God's plan being fulfilled in Lori's story.

I haven't a clue what the rest of God's plan consists of however I think this is just the beginning of a powerful long-term ministry. Lori's East Gate Story has touched many lives so far and has led many teary-eyed people to the saving grace of Jesus Christ.

I am greatly inspired by Lori's faith, work and resilience. After reading "Dirty Old Rags" I believe Lori's work will cause many to seek the way to those East Gates.

Bob Hines
Pastor Hazel Dell Baptist Church

This brief, God empowered biography of Lori's life will leave you moved to tears, in awe of God and His mercy and compassion, amazed by His gracious provision, and worshipping Him for who He is. All of this is clear in Lori's life and it is captured in this book. If you are someone who does not consider yourself a Christian, this story of a God who is near and who sees what you are going through, is well worth your time.

"We have been grateful and privileged to partner with Lori and East Gate for several years now. We are thrilled that God has seen fit to bless her and to work through her. It is exciting to watch Him continuously open doors for Lori and the East Gate Foundation, and it is challenging (in the best of ways) to see Lori live by faith in all of this. We commend this book to you for your reading, and we commend the East Gate Foundation for you to consider partnering with as well." – Justin J. Racca, *Lead Pastor*, Heaston Church (El Reno, Ok)

Justin J. Racca
Lead Pastor, Heaston Church

Lori Rush has inspired thousands of people to live a life with faith and purpose. Her story is one of power, love, and commitment to following whatever God calls her to do. Her entire family has a plan for eternity, and where they will meet each other when they get there. Lori is a person who truly sees no color, money, education, or status of a person but only their heart for following Christ Jesus.

As you read this book you will cry, laugh, and be challenged to do more than you ever thought possible. You will also find that miracles do happen, and when they do, we have to make a difference with the blessing we have been given. Lori is a wonderful friend who I admire and respect. The mission that God has given her is unique and amazing. At Pocasset First Baptist Church, Lori has an open invitation to speak at any time. So, let me challenge you to have her speak with your organization or church.

David Treadaway
Senior Pastor
Pocasset First Baptist Church
Pocasset, Oklahoma

What an inspiring and uplifting book this is! It is a book of miracles in the midst of an ordinary life with the setbacks and blessings that life brings. It is told with honesty and openness. Mostly, it is a book about gratefulness and obedience. Because of Lori's obedience to the vision God gave her, she has turned what could have been a tragedy into an open door for many, many people to hear the gospel and accept God's forgiveness and new life. You, too, can be changed by Lori's story. I highly recommend this book.

Ann Wegener
First Baptist Church, Minco

I've known Lori Rush for a number of years and first met her through a friend who knew her in Illinois and when she relocated to Yukon, OK to launch a new Christian childcare center. My first impression of Lori was that she was a "doer", not a talker and that she was a person of her word, a person of integrity and someone who could be counted on to follow thru. She turned out to be all of this and more. I lost track with her for a while, but heard she had experienced a traumatic, physical issue, but I had no idea how difficult this time was. In reading her detailed account in this book, it gives a look into the inner feelings and experiences of not only Lori, but her entire family. WOW! Very revealing, but the power comes when Lori points to Jesus as her sustainer and provider through it all.

The thing that this book did for me, most of all was to point me to the "life-changing" power of the blood of Jesus and sets a wonderful picture of the day that all who surrender to Jesus will experience; entering the gates of heaven. Whether it's the east, west, north or south gates, Lori's story gives us all the picture of what that day will be like...the day when we officially turn in our "dirty old rags" for a crown!

Thank you, Lori for your willingness to share your story of Jesus' transformational power and God's great love for us!

Jim Brooke
Retired Pastor and author,
'Becoming Families of FAITH'

Lori Rush is best defined by grace. God took something that was so awful, and yet made it so beautiful. He is good at doing that. Lori's story in "Dirty Old Rags" is inspiring, and it shows how great things can be accomplished through hard work and divine help. Lori's ministry has impacted several lives for the better. This story you are about to read will give insight to a special person and God's grace in action.

Kevin Sims
Minco Public Schools Superintendent

What can anyone say about Lori Rush? She is a woman whose life journeys have taken her through trials and tribulations, but she has remained strong through the strength of our Lord and Savior Jesus Christ. She is always giving of herself to others in need and never asking for anything in return. The love Lori has shown to others is endless. She is a Guardian Angel for me and many people whose lives she has touched. Lori thank you for being a wonderful, gracious and holy woman, but mostly for being my friend!

Ruth Littlejohn
Union City Correctional Center

"Dirty Old Rags" will keep you engaged with heartfelt, emotional, real life testimony! The book will encourage your faith in the grace, goodness, and provision of God in our everyday lives.

Mike Rutter
Prison Ministry Pastor

It is been a privilege and a blessing to call Lori Rush my friend for many years. I have been so amazed with her dedication to God and her work through the East Gate Foundation. So many lives have been touched and blessed because of her work!

This book chronicles her life from her childhood days in Illinois to moving to Oklahoma two different times and the adjustments she had to make with each move. Along the way is a roller coaster of emotions with family, with her Christian faith, and her health. She is very transparent as she shares her near-death experience and the struggles she faced emotionally and spiritually.

All of her life experiences have led Lori to begin an amazing journey with the East Gate Foundation. This ministry has helped so many people with physical, emotional and spiritual needs. God has called her to a ministry that is far outside her comfort zone… and, as you read this book…her story will inspire you with your own God sized calling that He has given you!

As I sat down to read Lori's story, I was so captivated by it that I couldn't put it down until I had finished. As you read it, keep the tissues handy and be prepared to be moved and inspired. I enthusiastically recommend *Dirty Old Rags*. You will be amazed with Lori, for sure…but even more amazed with our God!

Chuck Utsler
Retired Pastor and Director of Missions

As you pick up "Dirty Old Rags" and begin to read, you'll see God was at work in Lori's life at a very young age. No matter what circumstances she faced, He was always there watching over her. From being raised in a home with mental illness to surviving her own brain aneurysm, God was forging her into a tool He uses daily to point people to Heaven. Grab yourself a copy of her book and take an intimate journey through her life. You won't put it down until you're finished.

Lisa Kirkegard
Deedah's Cover of Love

If you are looking for a book to encourage your faith and amaze you with the goodness of God, you have found it. Lori has opened up her life and put it on display as a witness and testimony to God's love and His personal involvement in our lives.

Robin Brothers PhD, RN, CNE
Assistant Professor
College of Nursing
Oklahoma Baptist University
Women's Prison Ministry Leader

The words in this book are from a lady with a passion to share her testimony of Christ's love for others. At 9 years old, at a church alter, Lori Rush began her life journey of sharing and caring for those in need physically or spiritually. This journey has availed her many opportunities and rewards.

Whether trading M & Ms for left over hamburger buns and chips or riding with a Christian motorcycle club, Lori's testimony and Christian example has won the hearts of many.

You will want to read this book to see just where Christ brought Lori from "Dirty Old Rags" to where she is today.

Eric and Kathleen Coker
Missionaries

Lori and Jesus together make a great author. Some things really hit home for me.

I now have a greater desire to see all my family saved, three children, ten grandchildren, and eleven great grandchildren.

1. How firm and steadfast our faith in times of trial must be.
2. We must be attentive to listening for God's voice!
3. Your life reminds me of a scripture. All things work together for the good for those who love God.

I may never meet you down here but when I get to Heaven I'm going to hang around the East Gate. See you there.

Pastor Wendell Folsom
Gospel Tabernacle Church

"Dirty Old Rags" is the hauntingly compelling story of a woman called to action after tragedy, revealing the wonderfully loving, caring, and compassionate person she has become. Truly, Lori "walks the walk" in modeling Christian values through sharing her story and helping people in need find their way.

The Minco Millennium
301 West Main Street
P.O. Box 239
Minco, OK 73059

CHAPTER ONE

In the Beginning

I was born in Decatur, Illinois, in 1967 into a family with three siblings who were 10, 12, and 14 years older than me. My dad Stanley Mathias worked hard to provide for our family, oftentimes working two or three jobs. He encouraged and disciplined my siblings and me, and he gave the best "bear" hugs. My mom, Shirley, was the most beautiful, loving, gentle God-fearing mother I could ever ask for. As an adult, I realize the hard work and sacrifice my parents put forth in raising their children.

Shirley and Stanley Mathias

My first childhood memory was when I was about four years old. We lived in a mobile home in a small trailer park on West Harrison Street. Looking back, I believe that is when I first came to know of God's presence in my life. One day, I remember seeing two ambulance drivers fasten my mom to a stretcher while she was kicking and screaming. My dad didn't understand what was happening and was unable to handle her, so he had her committed for a psychiatric evaluation. That was the first time full-blown paranoid schizophrenia surfaced. This illness appeared every few years as I grew up.

That was the first time I remember feeling a knot in the pit of my stomach. With each recurrence of Mom's illness, I knew God was close. I learned about God from my mother and I felt His presence during those horrible episodes. He reaches us in the most mysterious ways.

My dad's sister Aunt Rose, her husband Uncle Paul, and my Grandma Mathias kept me at their house during Mom's hospital stay. Aunt Rose scrubbed me from head to toe the first night and each night thereafter. I wondered if I was too dirty to stay in their home. They bought me a new wardrobe full of dresses with lacy fringe and a new corduroy winter coat with a bonnet, new mittens and shiny shoes. (I must have looked like a rag doll to them when I showed up at their door.) I received a quick lesson in manners and etiquette. In my young mind, I thought it was my new home, and I would wear dresses every day, forever.

One day, I guess, four to six weeks later, my very thin, wild-eyed mom showed up. I remember how she bent down and reached her arms out to me. Although I was scared, I couldn't run to her fast enough. Momma, cracked and broken, loved me so very much. She would sometimes let me wear her silky nightgown when I didn't feel well. She would drive me to the doctor when I was sick. She always tucked me in at night and never failed to say, "I love you." I previously mentioned that my mother was the most beautiful, loving, and gentle God- fearing Mother.... I meant it! Let's just say when she was well, she was the best. She would teach me that I had a God who I could pray to and who would always be with me, regardless of circumstance.

God put people in my path who protected me, gave me stability and good loving experiences. I believe He was growing a seed of compassion in me. I feel certain that each of us could trace the moments God has touched our lives, if only we took the time to recognize them.

Dad was mentally and physically strong. Stubbornness proved to be a Mathias trait for all of us. He had a strong will and could not be budged when his mind was made up, but he had the most tender heart. Mom often said, "Your daddy would give us the world if he could." He raised us with expectations and integrity. He gave us advice even his grandchildren can still quote. He would say things like, "Don't rely on anyone else." "Don't judge anyone till you have walked in their shoes." "Never be afraid to try. The best way to fail is to never try. You'll be doomed from the start." "You got a dream you got to protect it! You want something go get it period." One of my favorites was, "Take can't out of your vocabulary." "One thing is certain you do not find life worth living. You make it worth living. A higher standard of thinking is a higher standard of living." Though life threw some curveballs sometimes we all knew Dad had our back no matter the project.

My oldest brother Gary met a gal by the name of Pamela Sue Mahoney. Pam lived in the mobile home across the street from us in the trailer court. She would oftentimes lure me across the street with suckers so that Gary would have to come get me. They were soon married in that little trailer, dressed in t-shirts and jeans. I spent a lot of time with them, and it wasn't long before they made me an Aunt at a very young age. I spent weekends and summers at their home. They were like my second set of parents, teaching me about life and spending time with me, especially when Mom and Dad weren't able.

Gary and Pam bought my first car, a Malibu. Once on a trip from Oklahoma to Illinois, Dad's car had engine trouble. Buying me my first car was Gary's way of making sure we were able to make the return trip home to Oklahoma. Dad would've never accepted such a gift. Gary was always looking out for us in ways a son shouldn't have to. He did it because that's the kind of guy he was.

My sister Sue married shortly after Gary. She married a black man by the name of Mickey. The early 70s proved to be a difficult time for acceptance of interracial marriages. My dad was reluctant in accepting this marriage. Eventually, however, he grew to love Mickey as a son of his own.

Gary, Roger, Dad, Mickey, Greg

I loved my Sissy and Mickey. They would often come to my rescue when things "got difficult" at home. Looking back, I know

Sis tried to give me a good childhood. Most times she would drive from the next town to get me in a car with a gas gauge that read "empty." She always managed, however, to scrape up enough change for our routine chips, dip and pizza. Some of my favorite memories are of times spent with her and her daughters, (my nieces) Heidi, Jeannette, Miki, and Latosha. Occasionally I would get to spend the weekend with her. We stayed up on Saturday nights crafting and watching Saturday Night Live, only I couldn't stay up past the beginning of the show. When it was time to return home on Sunday evenings, the knot in my stomach would reappear, along with a pounding heart. God gave me a sister who would turn out to be a life-long protector and encourager. She is truly a gift.

My youngest brother Greg would be the last to leave the nest. He would wrestle with me, give me piggyback rides and "Dad-like" hugs. He made me feel I was extra special. I recall times he would give Mom money for my school clothes. Sometimes he would take me to see a movie. He did things for me that an 18- year- old brother wouldn't typically do for his sister. He invested in my well-being, and he invested in me.

Once I was awakened to Mom screaming at my dad; there went that knot again. I could hear glass breaking; and I could feel the trailer shaking. Pictures were being torn off the walls in the living room and down the hallway past my room. Mom was screaming and crying. She suddenly became silent, and then I could hear my dad yelling at her. Finally, I heard Greg's truck pull up to the trailer, and he walked in and came straight to my room. I had my eyes closed as tight as I could when I heard the doorknob turning. I was so relieved to see that it was Greg instead of Mom or Dad. He came in, scooped me up in his arms, and held me tight for a long time. He reassured me that even though Mom and Dad were mad at each other in the moment, everything would be all right. I never wanted him to leave me, and he would stay until I fell asleep.

Greg stayed home for several more years. I feel certain he didn't stay because it was pleasant. In my heart, I know he wanted to be sure I would be okay. He sacrificed his early adulthood for me.

Thank you, Lord, for my siblings who you so strategically placed in my life.

Although my life may seem like it was full of hard times, there were seasons of laughter and good times, as well. Some of my best memories occurred when I was about nine years old. We moved into a two-story farm house in the country in Blue Mound, Illinois. My dad planted a huge garden. We had a chicken coop, a couple of sheep, a goat, cats, dogs, and guineas. We had a few pigs with the runt named Arnold. I had a horse named Star and a one-eyed rooster that looked sideways at you before he charged at you.

We had a big old wrap-around porch and a coal stove. The house was full of beautiful furniture that Dad bought from his Aunt Clara who lived in the Southwest, and there was an old upright piano. I had a slumber party once with about nine friends. We made indoor tents and played lots of music. We danced and played hide and seek. We ate pizza and laughed 'til we cried. I also, by this time in my life, had five nieces and a nephew. Greg still lived at home, and both my grandmothers were still alive. Life was fun. Life was good.

I found my way to the altar at the Blue Mound First Church of God at age nine. I remember I told Reverend Frank Hillman that I wanted to ask Jesus into my heart so I would know for certain that He would always be with me.

Mom taught a Sunday School class and often did puppet shows for the kids. During church services, Mom and Dad and I sat in the third row from the back at church. When we sang hymns, Mom would harmonize with me. She would write me sweet notes when I would get antsy. She always, it seemed, had a peppermint in her purse for me. Soon I began to take piano lessons and got to play

6

at church sometimes. If I could pick an age to be forever, it would be age nine.

I rode the school bus to school every day and sat next to my best friend, Terri, who lived a half mile down the road from me. If the wind was blowing just right, we could stand at our mailboxes and yell to each other.

One day Terri's mom came to talk to the bus driver before I got to my stop. They whispered and looked up at me in the overhead mirror. Elsie the driver told me, before I got off the bus, to go straight to my mom. I was scared and had that stupid old knot in my stomach. Something just didn't feel right that day.

Mom met me at the mailbox. As we were walking up the long driveway, she began to tell me that bad people kept pulling into the driveway and turning around. She was certain they would be back for us. She led me directly upstairs to her room, and we shut ourselves in. There we waited with a shotgun, waiting for those bad people. I was relieved to hear a car pull in and discover it was Greg. He would make everything right.

Through all of Mom's schizophrenic episodes, she still managed to teach me I had a God I could pray to, a God who would always be with me even when she couldn't be. I am so grateful that despite the turmoil that filled our household, I was never removed from my home.

I eventually became so afraid of that old two-story house that I would ask Mom to sit by the door when I had to use the restroom. There was a closet with a rickety lock, and it didn't shut well. Occasionally, it would pop open, so I was sure someone was living in there.

When I would have to go anywhere in the house, I would run as fast as I could past the coat closet, the basement door, the bathroom and the door to the upstairs, where the bedrooms were. The rooms in the house made a complete circle. As night came, I would add the windows to my list of places to avoid. I refused to go upstairs unless there was a family member up there. There was a banister on the top floor as you came up the stairs into a big open room that had two old closets like the one in the bathroom and the opening to an attic right above my bed.

It seems I never closed my eyes at night; rather, I would just fall asleep at some point. Greg's room was on the right of mine and Mom and Dad's room was on the left. I remember I would call for Mom to bring me another blanket as an excuse to get her to come into my room. Eventually, she let me sleep on a twin bed next to her bed on the nights Dad worked the third shift.

My bed was next to a window that allowed me to see past the roof to the driveway. The illumination from the light pole outside allowed me to see when Greg pulled in. Once I knew he was home, I felt safe enough to sleep.

Another huge fear I had was, what if I woke up and had to use the bathroom? I would have to go down the stairs, past the coat closet, past the basement door, into the bathroom with the closet door that sometimes popped open. Then to get back to my bed I would have to do a reverse run past all those creepy places.

I probably fueled my mom's schizophrenia as much as she fueled my fear of that house. As crazy as it was, I never feared her or felt unsafe in her presence. She taught me to pray.

Although my dad was a hard worker, he was never able to save any money. It seemed he could never "catch a break." Mental illness was treated differently in the 70s. There were fewer drugs available and at an astronomical cost. There were no programs to assist and insurance companies didn't want to cover the medicines Mom needed. I'm sure it had to be frustrating for Dad to be "married" to an illness that he hadn't signed up for.

I don't believe Mom ever had a breakdown before my fourth birthday. It seemed with every milestone in my life (i.e., eighth grade graduation, junior high, driver's license, marriage....) Mom's illness would reappear. We would, time and time again, struggle through, overcome, and life would be good again.

Treatment options available for Mom's illness included electric shock, institutional treatment and medicines that were too costly. When Mom began feeling better, she would stop taking her medicine, because it was so expensive. It wouldn't be long before she would again require hospitalization to rebalance her chemical need. Dad would get angry, expecting her to pull it together, and I believe he silently blamed her for not being successful with a business he tried to start. He never did understand her illness.

I never imagined those years would be molding me into who I am. Those episodes with my Mom grew my faith in God. The knot in my stomach would come many times, but I would immediately say, "God help me, I'm scared."

He always did.

CHAPTER TWO

Oklahoma Bound

When I was thirteen, the factory my dad worked at for years, Pittsburgh Plate Glass, laid off numerous employees including my dad. After the layoffs exceeded a couple of years, and no call back was anticipated, it was necessary for Dad to find new employment to provide for the family. Local opportunities were slim-to-none, so a decision was made to make a move to Oklahoma where there seemed to be a bounty of jobs available. We ended up moving and settled in a small town called Union City.

Dad was able to secure new employment, but it resulted in him working long hours. Dad primarily came home to eat, shower, and sleep. I remember getting permission to go home from school in the middle of the day to make sure Mom took her medication. There were many times I would go get groceries or do laundry. At fifteen I took a job at BJ Fast Stop to pay for things I needed. I would oftentimes leave the house early in the morning and not return until late in the evening. I rarely held any conversations with Mom, merely pecked her on the cheek as I came and went. This left her home alone a lot.

My teenage years brought out a rebellion of sorts in me. I began to party with all types of people and would find mischief wherever

I could. I learned to cuss like a sailor and was cold-hearted and short-tempered. I showed no respect for myself or others, and I felt life had no value. I often felt misunderstood and insecure in my way of thinking. I just didn't seem to fit in. This behavior continued from ages thirteen to twenty. I can see now that I was crying out. There was no Gary, no Sissy and no Greg. Regardless of my ill behaviors, my God remained with me even when I chose not to acknowledge him.

It's no wonder Mom had so many issues with her mental health during our stay in Oklahoma. I feel a tremendous guilt for my behavior during that time in our lives. It seems God would repeatedly tell me, "Lori, only through Christ are we perfect. Let it go and let me have your concerns once and for all. The world is broken and cracked and flawed, and you can only hurt on your own. It's only when Christ is in you that those "dirty old rags" are clean and white as new.

One evening at a party, I met a young man named Kenneth Rush. We began to spend a lot of time together. He seemed to enjoy spending time with me and accepted me for who I was, so I didn't have to pretend to be someone I wasn't. Kenny saw past my misbehaviors and seemed to see something good in me. I could bring him into my "circus" family at home, and still he wanted to be with me. He truly cared about me. He was what a friend of mine Linda Schutten would say, a "keeper".

CHAPTER THREE

Return to Illinois

We lived in Oklahoma from 1982 – 1988. Dad began having heart issues and in 1987 he went on a cardiac drug trial. That seemed to be the most viable solution for Dad, as Mom's illness prevented him from acquiring affordable health insurance. When the trial medications didn't improve Dad's circumstance, it was decided that my brothers should come move us back to Illinois. Although Dad certainly didn't like that decision, he agreed Mom should be closer to the older siblings. She would need someone to look after her should something happen to him. I suppose my recent erratic behaviors didn't suggest that I would be capable of filling any caregiver role.

Dad's heart issues surfaced shortly after Kenny and I met. I had finally found someone who cared about me, and I did not want to move for fear that I would not see him again. To my surprise, Kenny decided he would return to Illinois with us. Plans were made to make the move back to Illinois in February. God sent me someone who would love me and was willing to stand by my side through thick and thin. Thank you, God, thank you.

The trip to Illinois proved to be quite an adventure for Kenny and me. Everything we anticipated seemed fresh and new. We traveled home in his old El Camino with his cocker spaniel Buff in tow. The defroster in that old vehicle didn't work, so we had to pull over often to clean the inside of the windows. Oh, what fun it was to have winter again and our whole future together ahead of us.

I was able to find employment at St. Mary's Hospital. Ken worked as a guard for a company and served as a volunteer on the Decatur Police Department. It wasn't long before he was hired on full time at the Macon County Correctional Center. We were married the following year in April.

Ken and I-1989

I was so happy to be back in Illinois! I was home; and even though Ken missed his family, I vowed I would never leave my family again. That was that. My mind was made up!

Ken and I eventually moved into a house that my oldest brother purchased. It turned into a family project. My brothers and my dad helped build on three bedrooms and a new living room. I was in heaven: a new home, beautiful babies, two daughters and a son, great neighbors and my parents living right behind us. I finally had everything I ever wanted.

Dad passed away in 1994 at the age of sixty-four of a massive heart attack. I remember he once asked, as he was bouncing my son Kyle on his knee, if I could possibly want anything more in my life. If I had known his life would have been cut short, I would've certainly told him I wish I could have more time with him.

At the time of Dad's death, my mom was devastated. It wasn't long, however, before she began to turn her life around for herself. She began to save money and got back into church. It's been over twenty years and Mom has not had another mental breakdown. She is eighty-six now and mentally and spiritually stronger than ever. Tell me God is not good!

I honestly believe that death builds one's faith. We know with each passing of a loved one that Heaven is real. It must be! We rely on God's promise that he will provide us the opportunity to be reunited with loved ones that pass before us. His promise of everlasting life is at the forefront of our thoughts in those moments. When our grief begins to subside, it seems we forget about God's promise, or we become bitter and begin to question our faith. God's love isn't a part-time inclination; it is real and everlasting. He has non-judgmental love for each of us. Thank you, Lord, for the promise we have through you. Even as we draw our last breath, we can cry out to you, and you are merciful to save. Thank you for the many times you have wrapped your arms around my family and friends during our darkest hours. My faith grows with each moment I'm with you, voluntarily or not.

The year Dad died my mother realized she was missing something in her life that she had put aside entirely too long. She went back to church. She asked if Kasey, my oldest daughter, might walk with her the few blocks to church each Sunday. It wasn't long before I began to attend as well.

We attended services several years at that little church, Macon First Baptist. It was a time of faith building and preparing and growing. I would oftentimes play the piano during Sunday services. Many precious memories were made in that little church, and Sundays allowed Mom and me good quality time together. My family, except Lindsey, my youngest daughter, came to know the Lord there. I rededicated in that church; Lindsey accepted the Lord later.

I loved my life, and I spent many hours with Mom. I was active in my hometown, and I started a daycare in our home. I began to ask God to show me my purpose in His scheme of things. I suppose I should have been ready for His answer when I asked, so I wasn't totally blindsided by His direction. I loved being involved with the young children, so I went back to college to become director qualified. I had planned to build my own child care center right there in the town of Macon. I was going to call it "Country Bumpkin Christian Childcare Center." I would later learn that God's plan for me, however, was of a different calling.

Eventually, Ken accepted a position in a police department in a different town, Sullivan, which required that we move into their city limits within the year. I was not happy, by any means, with the thought of moving. My plans had been totally disrupted by this turn of events, but I soon recognized that God had a hand in this new venture. You can't ask for His direction and then not follow that direction. I argued with Him and thought to myself, I'll move, but I WON'T sell my home. I'll rent it out so when I'm ready, we can move back into it. Huge mistake! (Note: When God tells you to do something, don't try to wiggle your way around Him. Don't try to second-guess Him and try to create your own safety net; He is the only safety net you'll ever need.)

We found a big, beautiful, five-bedroom country home with a full basement in Sullivan. I thought I was, at least for the time being, in Heaven again.

This new town turned out to be a very dark place. It was as though a dark cloud hung over it. People were rude, pretentious Christians. My children's friends lived forty-five minutes away. Poor Kasey left behind all her friends. It turned out, however, we moved right across the street from a boy who would be Kyle's best buddy. Once I began working at my own daycare, "Little Helper's Christian Child Care Center," Lindsey became Kasey's responsibility.

Although the town itself was draining, my family grew a great deal in that strange place. We had stepped out of our comfort zone and began looking to God for direction and a sense of security. Ken and I took on newspaper routes from three to five every morning to make extra money. I began to seek God's direction and would pray the whole length of my route. Over and over I would ask God to use me and give me direction.

CHAPTER FOUR

The East Gate Story

One day when Kyle was 10 years old, he came sliding outside to the porch I was sitting on. "Momma, what does Heaven look like?"

I said, "Well, Bub, I know the Bible says there are streets of gold, and I know there is a big pearly gate. I'm not sure what all the Bible says about it. Go get your Bible, and we'll look it up."

I had never considered looking this up before, but Kyle found it very important that day. I knew there was a description, but I didn't know where. I knew there was a pearly gate, but I didn't realize there were gates on all sides of Heaven: North, South, East and West (Rev 21:21).

We spent the next few minutes looking at my wedding ring, talking about the streets of gold and different types of jewels one might see. Next, he asked me a question that would change my family and friends' lives. His big blue eyes were worried. He asked me, "How will I find you there?"

For years, I have been protective of my children. If we went to Walmart, "This is where you meet me if you get lost." When we went grocery shopping, "You stay here if you get separated from me." At the park, "We'll meet at the swings."

I said, "Bubba, can you pick a gate, and remember it even if you live to be 100 years old?"

"Yeah" he said.

"All right, pick a gate, and if I get to Heaven before you do, I'll be waiting at that gate. If you get there first, you wait for me there, okay?"

I knew my child needed Heaven to be real, and I wanted him to know his whole life, I would meet him there, and I was going to be expecting him there. He picked the East Gate. Over the next seven years, I would watch him playing a video game, and I would ask, "You remember what gate?"

"Yup, East Gate!"

Sometimes when I'd tuck him in, or if I saw him deep in thought, I'd ask, "Hey, Bub, you remember our meeting place?"

"Yup, East Gate!"

I thank God every day that he allowed Kyle and me to share that moment on that big old front porch. That conversation will, one day, lead my children, my husband, and all my family to that heavenly meeting place. The promise to Kyle grew my faith that day.

REVELATION 21: 11-27 NEW INTERNATIONAL VERSION (NIV)

21[11] It shone with the glory of God, and its brilliance was like that of a very precious jewel, like a jasper, clear as crystal. [12] It had a great, high wall with twelve gates, and with twelve angels at the gates. On the gates were written the names of the twelve tribes of Israel. [13] There were three gates on the east, three on the north, three on the south and three on the west. [14] The wall of the city had twelve foundations, and on them were the names of the twelve apostles of the Lamb.

[15] The angel who talked with me had a measuring rod of gold to measure the city, its gates and its walls. [16] The city was laid out like a square, as long as it was wide. He measured the city with the rod and found it to be 12,000 stadia in length, and as wide and high as it is long. [17] The angel measured the wall using human measurement, and it was 144 cubits thick. [18] The wall was made of jasper, and the city of pure gold, as pure as glass. [19] The foundations of the city walls were decorated with every kind of precious stone. The first foundation was jasper, the second sapphire, the third agate, the fourth emerald, [20] the fifth onyx, the sixth ruby, the seventh chrysolite, the eighth beryl, the ninth topaz, the tenth turquoise, the eleventh jacinth, and the twelfth amethyst. [21] The twelve gates were twelve pearls, each gate made of a single pearl. The great street of the city was of gold, as pure as transparent glass.

[22] I did not see a temple in the city, because the Lord God Almighty and the Lamb are its temple. [23] The city does not need the sun or the moon to shine on it, for the glory of God gives it light, and the Lamb is its lamp. [24] The nations will walk by its light, and the kings of the earth will bring their splendor into it. [25] On no day will its gates ever be shut, for there will be no night there. [26] The glory and honor of the nations will be brought into it. [27] Nothing impure will ever enter it, nor will anyone who does what is shameful or deceitful, but only those whose names are written in the Lamb's book of life.

CHAPTER FIVE

Last Move

E ventually, Ken and I were called back to Oklahoma. My fervent decision to stay in Illinois went out the window when my Pastor called one day and said, "Lori, I'd like you to consider moving to Oklahoma and start a Christian Day Care/Preschool at the time I begin a new ministry." (I thought there was no way I was moving. I had already made my plans, and they did not include moving back to Oklahoma.) When I asked where they had planned to settle down, my Pastor replied, "Yukon." When he shared this bit of information, I felt sick for a moment. Yukon was a mere thirty miles from the area where Kenny was raised, and he and I met. I knew right then that we were indeed making the move.

We moved back to Oklahoma in a blizzard in December 2003. We moved into an old farmhouse in Minco once occupied by Kenny's grandparents.

Shortly before returning to Oklahoma, Mom had a bad car wreck back in Illinois. She misjudged a turn and slid off an exit ramp. She was trapped in her car and went un-noticed for several hours. Eventually a motorist traveling the same route caught a glimpse of her overturned car. She was shaken but not seriously injured. She would soon be admitted into a nursing home for rehabilitation. Oh, how I hated not being closer to her. To add insult to injury, the Pastor we had made the move for turned out to be totally different than we expected. The plans for the home I kept in Illinois, even though I knew God intended for me to sell it, turned out to be quite disastrous as well. The moment we left Illinois the renters decided to stop paying the rent. From appearances, they allowed their children to run rampant and cause a great deal of damage to the interior. My beautiful home was, in fact, destroyed and left us facing foreclosure. We ended up doing a "short sale" to my brother Gary. I began to question the decision in moving back to Oklahoma. What were we doing?

My children initially had a hard time with the move to Oklahoma. I remember the first time we drove down 81 South between Minco and Pocasset. There was a farmer ahead of us riding his oversized tractor. He pulled over to the side of the road and motioned us to go ahead and pass him. The kids were frightened. "What is he waving at us like that for?" Ha-ha! In Illinois, people would gesture while driving for completely different reasons.

When my oldest daughter, Kasey, realized she could ride Grandpa's horse down Main Street, through the Dairy Boy, and get a milkshake without anyone batting an eye, she was sold on Oklahoma. Eventually she would become a Rodeo Ambassador for Minco and raise thousands of dollars for the club and later lead her own drill team, the Red Dirt Revival Equestrian Drill Team. Maybe God's intent in directing our move wasn't intended to just give direction in my life.

With all the negative things happening with Mom, our home, my daycare, I felt justified in being angry with God. I completely and purposely turned away from the church. I refused to speak to God, and I was not going to listen to or follow any direction He might offer. Looking back, I realize that was a dangerous place to be in, but at the time I did not care.

I assumed the position of a Childcare Director for a few years and then no longer felt compelled to work in that capacity. I longed to return to the healthcare industry and would soon seek employment at one of the hospitals. I was fortunate to secure a job with a wonderful Integris orthopedic surgeon, Dr. Michael Davoli. I absolutely loved my new position.

Ken and I kept busy with our family, as all three kids were involved in various extracurricular activities: rodeos, ballgames, band, and cheer. There seemed to be something to do and places to be all the time.

Thanksgiving-Lindsey, Kasey and Kyle

One day it seems, I woke up and felt a sense of unhappiness and bitterness. I felt I needed something more in my life, but I couldn't put my finger on it, so I chalked it up to my age. At forty, I thought perhaps I was going through perimenopause. I felt like I was surrounded by idiots, and I began to get angry with anyone who looked my way. I found fault in any and everything others did and would be quick to begrudge and judge them. I began to find fault in my co-workers and friends. I became quick-tempered and oftentimes felt like "clearing a table" or throwing something.

Because of my behaviors, my family suffered and began to "walk on eggshells," uncertain of how I might respond to any given situation. I created a tense atmosphere in every aspect of my life.

There were even times I began to question my marriage. It seems, no matter how I tried, I couldn't acquire a sense of happiness that I longed for. I eventually began to push family away. If I felt the least bit criticized or belittled, I immediately cut the source of it out of my life. I even had a couple of "come to Jesus" meetings, but the turmoil I was feeling was continuing to consume me. I couldn't comprehend or control what was taking place.

As a last resort, I searched for a doctor that could help calm my inner being. I thought perhaps I had inherited Mom's illness and might need professional help. It was eventually determined that while I was highly emotional and moody, I was not mentally ill. There was no definitive solution to my condition. Looking back, it's clear that the beginning of my mood changes were the beginning signs of a serious health issue that would soon come to light.

CHAPTER SIX

The Rupture

ঔড়

It was a Sunday evening when my family and I were getting ready for bed. For the parent of three children, that meant making sure each one had all their homework done, any papers signed that needed to be, money for lunches or other necessities, clean clothes, two shoes, and two matching socks laid out for the next morning.

I thank God, that on that night, I had told all my children that I loved them. It could have been, "Knock it off in there!" "Go to sleep, not another word!" Thank you, Lord, for the loving words I spoke that night.

My husband and I turned in about ten o'clock. The next thing I knew, I was abruptly awakened by Kenny shaking me and yelling, "Lori, wake up." I felt as though I had just closed my eyes and fallen asleep. He said I had what appeared to be a seizure, became very stiff and shook violently. Well, if that wasn't enough to scare me, the look on his face was. I felt nauseated while the reality of what he said shook me to my core. I never had seizures; I never even had headaches. The only thing that had been out of the ordinary was that horrible attitude and temper that I had recently been displaying.

I sat up and Ken said, "I'm calling an ambulance." I begged him not to call. When you call an ambulance in Minco, you get a dozen volunteer firemen and police in your house. He sat there for a moment, and when I asked what he was thinking, he said, "I really want you to go to the hospital." Again, I felt as though I was going to be sick. Our bedroom was on the back porch of our old farm house, so Ken quickly opened the back door. I leaned over Grandma's flower bed and I vomited... hard! I felt and heard a loud pop in my head and instantly felt warmth in my head, top to bottom.

There were many things that instantly came to mind. I thought I was going to die! Ken will be by himself. Did I just get hit with a sledge hammer in the back of my head? The only thing I cried out in my mind was, "SAVE ME!" I cried out to God when I was most vulnerable, because in that moment, I felt my life was near an end, and I needed to know, again, that God was by my side.

I told Kenny I'd go to the hospital, but I didn't want an ambulance, so he raced outside to start the truck. I tried to put socks and shoes on, but I felt clumsy and awkward and weak. When Kenny returned to the house, he helped with the socks and shoes, and then helped me out to the truck. I felt, oh, so weak. As we were leaving the house, Kenny leaned into Kasey's room and said, "I'm taking Momma to the Emergency Room." I heard Kasey and Lindsey hurriedly asking him questions, but they seemed so distant that I couldn't hear what they were saying.

I have rarely seen Kenny lose his cool, but as we drove toward Integris Canadian Valley Hospital, I had to tell him to slow down. We hadn't made it to the highway before I started vomiting again. This time it was very uncontrolled and without warning. Over and over I vomited. There can't naturally be room for that much inside one person. At some point, I sprayed the entire inside of the windshield and Kenny had to pull over somewhere between Minco and El Reno. He ran around to my door and had to take his hand to turn my head, so I could vomit outside the truck. I remember hearing my voice, as if it were someone else saying, "I can't turn my head." Looking back, I don't know how I was alert enough to tell Kenny to slow down once we were close to Exit 136 which would lead us to the hospital.

I remember the volunteer that was working at the West Entrance of the hospital that evening. She brought out a wheelchair for me. One of my most memorable moments of that night was how comforted I felt when she touched my shoulders, bent down and said, "We've got you. You are going to be okay."

I was taken into a new area of the hospital that I had never seen before, and I was immediately sent for a CT scan. I remember having trouble transferring from the bed to the table because my body was still trying to vomit. I do not know how the technician was able to obtain any readable scans.

Moments later, the Integris Canadian Valley Emergency Room doctor, Dr. Stigler, came in with a scan in his hand that showed blood all around my brain. He said, "What you have is a sub arachnoid hemorrhage versus a ruptured brain aneurysm. People who have a ruptured brain aneurysm don't walk into ER like you just did. Thirty-five percent have lost something major, like speech, movement on one side of their body, or are unconscious or in a coma. The other sixty-five percent of brain aneurysm ruptures are fatal." He then told us I would be transferred to the on-call neurologist that night, most likely for a coiling procedure.

The terror was settling in now. They began getting me in a gown and giving me medication to help with the nausea. I asked to use the restroom, but they said from here on out I would not be allowed to sit or stand up until the source of the bleeding was found. I would have to be catheterized.

I made eye contact with Kenny. I was afraid of what was happening and thought I was surely going to die. Although he tried to hide his concern there was a sadness in his eyes that let me know death was a very real possibility. My life was in jeopardy and tomorrow could not be promised.

When the medicine started to have a calming effect on me, I dozed off and on. I remember the doctor came in explaining that he was working to transfer me to another hospital as the neurologist on call didn't perform the coiling procedure. He fervently continued to make calls and wait for answers. It took several hours before he finally returned and said if we didn't get an answer soon, I would be medi-flighted to Dallas. Finally, the answer came. St. Anthony's Hospital had a surgeon who could perform the coiling procedure.

The next few hours were a blurry whirlwind of events. An ambulance came for me, and a nurse ran out to the bay alongside me, holding my hand. I was so frightened. I asked her if she would pray for me. She assured me she would. Prayer never felt more important than it did at that moment. Kenny drove our truck behind the ambulance in my transfer to St. Anthony's.

I remember during the ambulance ride, I repeatedly thanked EMT's. I kept saying, "Thank you for helping me." At some point, I was more concerned of being afraid than anything. If I admitted I was scared, I would lose control of myself, and I knew it. My feeling of gratitude lasted throughout my entire health crisis. I have never ceased to be thankful.

Once we arrived at St. Anthony's, the wait for a room in the ICU seemed an eternity. My focus, however, was on hope that the residing neurologist would be able to fix this.

I kept thinking about Kasey; she was the one who would know how serious this was. She's the most tenderhearted person I've ever known, and surely this would be killing her. Lindsey was sleeping with Kasey that night and was probably still sound asleep. I didn't know if Kyle even knew where I was. Dad texted Kasey occasionally, giving her updates.

The following morning, I was moved into the ICU where Kenny and I waited for the neurologist to come in. Once he arrived, he said he would order a cerebral arteriogram to try to locate the source of the bleeding. Once the source was identified, he would decide if it needed a coiling procedure or a clipping. He said it was important for me to stay flat and for my blood pressure to stay low until the bleed was located and repaired.

I waited until 7 a.m. the following day to call off work. I was alert enough to ask Ken for his cell phone and called Denise Roper, the Specialty Clinic Director, at Integris Hospital, my place of employment. I told Denise I wouldn't be in for a couple of days, as I was in the hospital with either a cerebral hemorrhage or a ruptured brain aneurysm. I can still recall the startled disbelief in the sound of her voice. "What? You are where? A couple of days?!"

Pastor Steve Shelhamer and his wife Pam from Minco First Baptist Church came right away and prayed with Kenny and me. There has never been a prayer that meant more to me than the one I heard Pam speak asking our Heavenly Father to stop the bleeding and save my life. I was humbled to have someone come pray for me, and I was additionally humbled to have been alert enough to hear that prayer. I could feel the prayers going up for me. That feeling was overwhelming and provided immediate comfort to me.

CHAPTER SEVEN

A Miracle Unfolding

My kids were heavy on my mind and I really needed to see them. Pastor Shelhamer offered to pick them up from school and bring them to the hospital. Lindsey would need to be picked up from the junior high and Kyle from the high school. Kasey had already graduated and had been texting her dad, so she drove herself. I'm not sure what Steve told my kids on the way to see me, but I believe they were told to try to remain calm so as not to upset me, or they might not be able to stay in ICU with me.

My first child to come in was my oldest daughter, my sweet Kasey, my eighteen-year-old. My most tenderhearted was so broken. She came straight to me and laid her head on my chest. God must have been guarding me, because I only heard her weeping quietly, but later Kasey said she sobbed loudly and uncontrollably. I thought, God, I can't do this. Please don't make me say good-bye to my baby girl. Then I looked down and saw she had written something in black marker on the tops of her hands. I recognized what she had done. In junior high and high school, when something was heavy on her heart, she would find scripture that spoke to her and write it on her hands. She would read it over and over, and then when negative thoughts began to surface, she would read the verse, replacing those negative thoughts with positive ones. I didn't realize that she was currently practicing Philippians 4:8:

"Finally, brothers and sisters, whatever is true, whatever is noble, whatever is right, whatever is pure, whatever is lovely, whatever is admirable-if anything is excellent or praiseworthy-think about such things."

My heart was comforted when I saw the writing. I thought, my baby girl is going to be okay if I must go. I held her hand and said, "We know where to get our strength from, don't we?" She sobbed as she nodded.

Next in was Lindsey. My dark-haired, sassy little freckled-faced beauty stood off in the corner. I could tell she was afraid to talk to me. I could see her lip quiver just a little as she came close to me. She said, "It's going to be okay, Mommy. God's going to take care of you." Kenny smiled at me and winked from across the room. She knew who was in control. I thought, thank you Lord for making it simple enough for a child to understand. Again, my heart was comforted by this show of faith. I knew my church family would pull her close if I did have to go, and they would make sure she knew God did take care of me.

Now it's Bub's turn. I always smile when he walks into a room. Now, he's not Bub, he's Kyle. He's six feet tall and able to drive himself. He came in and sat down next to me and held my hand. I needed him to know the truth. I said, "Bub, this is really serious."

He replied, "I know, Momma, but I remember East Gate."

What he said at that moment burned to the very center of my heart. The room was so quiet you could hear a pin drop. As I looked around the room, I realized my three children and my husband, and I all knew Christ! We had a meeting place, and we had been talking about it for years! The peace I felt at that moment was indescribable! I knew if I left this life today, it would be alright. I knew one day I would be reunited with them again for all eternity.

I remember thinking, God, if I make it through this, I need to let others know how important it is to talk to your family and friends ahead of time. Everyone needs to know about Heaven and the one way to get there. We prepare for a lot of things as we go through life. We plan for college and retirement. We plan for the worst by insuring almost everything. Shouldn't we plan for our afterlife as well? I was forty-two years old when I had an aneurysm rupture. I didn't even know I had an aneurysm. My point is, tomorrow isn't promised. It's important that we talk about the way to achieve an everlasting life and that only way is Jesus Christ.

Later that day, I would go in for the procedure to locate the source of the bleed. I was humble and thankful. I was anxious to have the procedure done. The clock was ticking, and I hadn't, thus far, had a stroke or any significant occurrence. Kenny and the kids stayed with me. When the nurse started an IV, Kyle just about went down. Kenny caught him before he passed out. Suddenly, the seriousness of what was happening again set in. They gave me hugs, and I went in for what would be the first of many cerebral arteriograms.

The room was cold and bare. The arteriogram was started in the groin, and a wire was fed to the brain through an artery. I felt like I was going to pass out. The team would tell me to hold my breath, and they would take a picture to see if they could tell where the artery was bleeding. During this procedure the nurse who was standing behind me kept putting her hands on my shoulders assuring me, I wasn't alone. (That comforting touch meant a great deal to me, as I'm sure it does to others.) The procedure seemed to last hours.

The next thing I recall was a red-headed nurse coming into my ICU room and telling my family and me that my vital signs looked good, and they couldn't find any source of any bleed from the arteriogram. The nurse said this was good news. She continued to say I would most likely be epileptic like her son. She tried to explain that lots of people have epilepsy and manage quite well. After she explained I was going to be fine, my family decided to head home while my niece Shalisa stayed behind. After my family left, while the nurse was telling us more about her son, in walked the internist to follow up with the results of the procedure. He overheard what the nurse had been saying about how I would be fine and stated, "This is still a very dangerous situation you are in. They did not find the source of the bleed, but they WILL try again. The brain doesn't like to have blood surrounding it, as in your case. It becomes very angry and goes into vasospasms at which time makes you susceptible to a stroke." I looked over at Shalisa and she asked, "So my family should still be concerned? That nurse just sent them home." He replied, "We are definitely not out of the woods." Shalisa immediately called Kenny with this new information.

My first inclination in hearing the doctor's concern was to chastise that nurse for giving hope to patients when she had no right to do so. I also heard that same nurse later berating the patient to the left of me. When the patient was moaning and talking out of her head, that nurse stated that she would not tolerate all that noise. She is the same nurse that stressed to my family they would have to leave if it got noisy or if my blood pressure went up. While I would have normally called her on her behavior, I thought if I was anything but thankful for the miracle I had already begun to receive, I would be deemed ungrateful, so I just began to pray.

There were many things throughout the stay that I had to surrender to God. It was day one and my first lesson. As I write now, the thankfulness is causing me to tear up. Thank you, Lord, for staying with me.

Every day we would try the arteriogram, but with no luck.

The H1N1 flu struck very hard while I was in ICU. The hospital wasn't allowing any visitors into the ICU except my husband. He still had to work every day to keep our household going, so I spent a lot of time alone.

There was a hospitalist who came in daily to see me. He stood out among everyone else, simply because he would touch my feet while standing at the end of my bed. A human touch and a prayer can do a great deal to soothe a broken spirit. There is nothing more comforting than knowing you are not alone.

I spent a week at St. Anthony's without gaining any knowledge of how or why my aneurysm came to be. I was told I would be discharged at the end of the week. My vital signs were all good, and they could not find the source of the bleed that occurred in my brain.

The hospitalist came in and said to me, "Are you going to be okay going home?" In my mind I thought, I can't believe they are sending me home; I'm going to die at home! I was so afraid to be anything but grateful that God had shown me favor that I wasn't about to show any negativity to anyone. I told the internist, "If I have to go home and pray every morning and every moment in between, 'Lord don't let me die in front of my children', then that is what I'll do; I'm going to be okay."

As the hospitalist left my room, I could hear his heels clicking down the hallway and then I heard a cell phone ring. The clicking stopped, and he reappeared at my door. He said, "You're not going to believe this. You just finished telling me God was going to be with you every moment. I just received a phone call from a world renowned neuroradiologist who says he's been working on a new way of finding aneurysms, and he would like to take your case. He said if you can come in the next couple of hours, he'll see you. Is this something you'd like to do?"

God was working behind the scenes on my behalf even when I thought no one was. Of course, I said, "Yes!"

I went by ambulance to Mercy Hospital. I felt hope, and for the first time someone who knew my case felt they could help me. Cerebral arteriograms were performed on me every day for a week. In layman terms, the doctor would run a wire through the groin up through the brain and spray "neuro-juice" over my brain. This would calm the vasospasms I had been having since the rupture, and let them take pictures, possibly spotting a difference from one picture to the next to ascertain where the artery had blown open.

Apparently, the artery burst and then fell back down, appearing as though no rupture had occurred at all. If it weren't for the vasospasms and all the blood around the brain, the scan would've appeared normal. I was so afraid each time I would go into this huge procedure room. Everyone would walk behind a wall with a window, so they could view the pictures. I was then told to hold my breath, and I would close my eyes. I could feel something in my head, and I could literally see a mapping of my brain while my eyes were closed. It was somewhat like rubbing your eyes for a long time and seeing stars when you stop.

Every day after the negative test, I would be required to lie still on my back for a couple of hours before they could take the sheath out. I believe lying still was the entire reason I was there. In hind sight, there were many lessons and revelations in those moments. God was able to speak to me as I was forced to be still and listen to him, thus allowing me to see His hand move up-close and personal.

First, I needed to be humbled. I became aware that each day that passed without resolution increased my chances of having a stroke or dying. I had already made it beyond the critical first twenty-four hours. How much more time would God allow me? I know the prayers offered up for me allowed me God's saving grace. I can't explain, but I felt those prayers in my soul. I heard rumors of churches praying for me and my family. One of the other Minco churches sent a prayer blanket to me which I held close through each procedure.

CHAPTER EIGHT

Lessons Along the Way

God made me realize something about myself around day eight of my hospital stay. It's funny how lying flat on your back on death's doorstep for days will break a stubborn and judgmental person's perspective of people. I have a newfound respect for love and compassion.

There was a young woman who was an acquaintance of our family. She lived nearby and was someone I considered "dirty." I didn't agree with how she lived, how she kept her house, or how she raised her children. I felt she surrounded herself with drama and filth. She also had a physical defect. Having described her the way I just did, you must know I thought I was better than she was. I didn't want my children around her, even though my children thought she was a very kind woman. They liked her daughter, who had the same physical imperfection as her mom. I showed this young woman absolutely no compassion, and I was totally indifferent to her child.

One day after the flu quarantine was lifted at the hospital, while I was alone and Kenny was at work and the kids were all in school, in walked this young woman. She sat right on the edge of my bed and picked up my hand. I began to weep; I had never been so ashamed in my life. She said, "I came to tell you I've been praying for you, and I have my church praying for you as well." I began to cry even harder. "Thank you." was all I could get out. We sat holding hands, and even when I would doze off for a few moments, she never left me. She sat with me for what seemed to be an entire afternoon. She never left me, not once. Finally, she said, "Lori, I must leave now, but I will keep praying for you, and if I get some more gas money, I'll come back and sit with you again. I love you friend, bye." She loved me unlike any friend I had known. She truly loved me, so she came and just sat. It's all she had to give, a very precious thing, her time. I had been so judgmental and as far from "Christian" as I could have been.

The lesson I learned from her behavior and one I'm most grateful for still makes me cry. It is easy to love your church family and your very own family and friends. It is Christ-like to love everyone, even those who may not look like you think they should or those whose lifestyle is different from your own. Love could be the greatest healing power there is here on earth. It must be why Christ said so many times to do just that. I witnessed first-hand what exactly was meant by the expression of "the power of love".

Another lesson I learned was grace. Several months before the aneurysm, I had developed a temper and intolerance to people. It took something very small for me to be done with them. It could be the tone of a voice, an unfair action, or I could just be tired of their character. I wasn't speaking to my sister-in-law Pam at the time and refused to speak to her on the phone. She would call Kenny on his cell phone to find out how I was doing. When she would ask to speak to me, I'd tell him I didn't want to talk. The fact was I was stubborn and refused to let her in.

One evening, Pam called and talked to Kenny for quite a while. The look on his face was more serious than usual. He brought me the phone again and told me Pam wanted to talk to me. Once again, I refused. I didn't want to talk. This time he pushed my hand down and put the phone to my ear. She just wanted to tell me she loved me. She didn't want anything to happen to me and she wanted me to know she loved me and was sorry for whatever she had done that had upset me.

It was the tone of her voice that made me realize how horrible I had been, refusing to allow someone to be human and flawed. I had been refusing forgiveness to someone, and here I lay, receiving grace and mercy even though I myself was human and flawed. Christ died for me and my sins. My hatefulness and stubbornness wouldn't allow me to offer forgiveness to my sister until my hand was forced. His grace shone even brighter for me with each day after.

I was becoming exhausted from fasting every day for the testing; my arteriogram site was black and blue and swollen. I had been catheterized for days; I wanted a shower; I wanted to know that this was coming to an end. To be honest with myself, I was prepared to go on to my heavenly home if God would only take me.

My mother-in-law had always been near and dear to me. She had always been my rock. Somehow, over the few months before the rupture, I had myself convinced that she didn't need or deserve my love. I spewed out a great deal of venom toward her in the six months prior to my aneurysm about meaningless "things," yet here she was spending her time with me while Kenny was at work. Late one evening, she sat close to me and held my hand for a bit. I felt all the emotions that I had for her swell up in me. I knew I had said things to her that were inappropriate. I had allowed her to make me mad, and I unleashed twenty years of feelings on her. Finally, I told her I was sorry for the way I had been treating her. We both cried. How I ever thought I was sovereign enough to withhold forgiveness to someone, I'll never know. How many times would I need this lesson? God forgives us without hesitation, yet I could easily make someone "pay" if I felt they did me wrong.

The people who left the greatest impression on me during my stay weren't necessarily the nurses or doctors or neurology teams. It was the volunteers that took me from test to test. It was the housekeeper who would pause to listen when there was no one else around. Even the workers in the cafeteria would encourage my family. I began to realize each of our roles in life is like a piece to a puzzle. We can't see the whole picture when we stand alone. It is only when we are focused on serving the Lord and working together and loving each other that all things ARE possible. His ability to work through us has no measure. We allow His love to be seen on a greater level when we all work together…Miraculous!

One day I received a phone call from my momma. She asked, "Lori, did I tell you enough that I love you when you were growing up?" I replied, "Oh, yes, Momma, you did. You always made me feel loved. You taught me who Christ was. That was the greatest love of all.

During my hospital stay, family and friends called to check on my well-being. Several people, church members, friends, and family, came to visit. There were, however, some special people, whom I can never repay who came. My sister and my boss Denise spent endless hours with me, even as I slept. I thank God for them always.

Every day after the arteriogram, someone would come in and tell me they were unsuccessful locating the source of the rupture. One particularly glorious day was different. My brain surgeon Dr. Fadi Nasr came in, bent down to see me face-to-face, and introduced himself. He said, "We found it! The coiling procedure is not an option for this aneurysm rupture. We'd like to do an open craniotomy with a clipping on Tuesday. The aneurysm was behind your right eye." Having been told this news, you would think I would have felt a great sense of relief. Unfortunately, to my surprise, when Dr. Nasr smiled, he revealed a full set of braces. I also noticed he had freckles on his nose. I thought, now for sure I'm going to die.

It had been over two weeks since my admission into the hospital. Now that they had located the source of the bleed, I was finally allowed to sit up and have something to eat.

I had been given more statistics than just the survival rate of the rupture. My neurosurgeon gave statistics again when he came in to discuss the open craniotomy and clipping, I would be having in a couple of days. He said it might be one hundred and twenty days after surgery before I would be ready to relearn how to use some small motor skills. I may need therapy to learn to talk or walk again. I would then work toward having a part-time job and would eventually be able to lead a productive life in society again. I wish I'd had the faith to say, "Dr. Nasr, you must not know my God; He doesn't go by a book of statistics." I asked instead, "Have you done this procedure before?"

You would think that we would all be excited for surgery. My worst nightmare used to be from a show I watched as a child. A chimpanzee craniotomy was taking place and his brain was being eaten as a delicacy in some foreign land. Now, I could not shake that image.

The day of the surgery, several of us met in the holding area and prayed for me. I asked Kenny if he thought I might see my dad while I was in surgery. I wasn't going to be scared or say it out loud for fear what I spoke would come true. It must have been then that I received the "happy-to-be here medicine" that I hear about at work.

I remember being wheeled into the operating room and people introducing themselves to me. I remember thanking each of them for helping me, for saving my life. After surgery was over, the first voice I heard was Dr. Nasr asking, "Lori, it's Dr. Nasr, do you know where you are?" I had secretly learned the address of the hospital during my stay, as I had been asked that very question every day since my admittance to the hospital. Every day I would reply when asked, "Mercy, ICU." This time before even opening my eyes, I automatically answered, "3400 West Memorial Road." I don't know for sure, but I imagined Dr. Nasr smiled. As it turned out, that young man was a brilliant surgeon, and today I send patients to him every chance I get.

When I woke after I was back in ICU, all I could think about was Kasey. My sister was with me, and she had been told I was to have no stimulation for twenty-four hours, but when I awoke, I immediately asked for my phone and called Kasey. She answered, and I said, "Hi, Kasey!" She said, "Mom! Oh, my gosh, I love you! I can't believe you are calling!"

Thank you, Lord, for this beautiful gift too wonderful for words. His praise was already on my lips.

There was very little postoperative pain involved for me. I was up walking the next day with some help from the nurse. I felt very off balance. I asked my sister for my purse and balanced the checkbook. Ha-ha! It certainly felt good to know I could still function normally.

Two days after surgery, I was moved into a regular room and told I would be going home in a day or two. That is where the major meltdown happened.

At some point during this ordeal, I began looking toward heaven as being the end of this journey. While I loved my husband and my children more than anything, my soul longed to go home to Jesus. When I got the news that I was going back to my earthly home, I was in total disbelief. This is not how it was supposed to go! Statistics dictated that I wasn't supposed to make it! I was left alone for a little while and couldn't stop crying. I asked for pastoral care to come.

I pictured myself as a small child. I had been sitting on my Heavenly Father's lap for days on end, drawing closer to Him, trusting Him to hold me every moment of this trial. To be taken down from His lap and told I could now go home? To God, I must have looked like a small child throwing a temper tantrum.

That evening, I couldn't sleep. I couldn't stop crying. The nurse said the many emotions I was feeling were probably due to the steroids I had been on. I thought my emotion was due to thinking I was going to my Heavenly home, and now I was not.

As I lay there weeping later that same evening, a foreign woman came in to get my trash. She sat next to me and held my hand and asked if she could help. I sobbed, telling her my story of how I would soon be returning home to my family, but I was so sad that I wouldn't be going home to be with Jesus. She looked saddened herself. She said she was married with two small boys. The boys both had severe cases of autism and couldn't sit still or listen. Her husband was abusive to her and her children. She said she cried every night because she longed to return to her native home in Iraq. She was, however, concerned that should she return to be with her mother, the children might be put in harm's way. She voiced her concern that when they got to the Iraqi airport her children would probably not listen and would be gunned down if they didn't do as the guards ordered. She said, "I just keep praying and keep going. One day, I will get home."

I felt horrible for her. Here I lay crying like a big baby because I was given this second chance at life, and she sat crying because she wasn't. She held my hands and prayed for both of us. I was never so humbled as I was at that moment. I never saw her after that night. I believe she was sent to be my comforter and give me greater perspective.

I never looked back for those feelings. I know now, in my heart, that I was allowed my second chance at life so I could complete a work with East Gate, a work that had begun several years earlier when Kyle and I had our conversation on that porch. I'm thankful every day that God allows me to be an instrument in sharing His promise of a life everlasting. I also realize there are a lot of people I love who don't know Jesus. I don't want to leave this life on Earth until the last person has come to know Him.

In the months that followed, I came to know many cancer patients and their families. I often share this first-hand experience with them about how, when death seems imminent, you become less afraid. Your soul starts longing to go where it truly belongs. It's a beautiful thing, and once you focus on Heaven, you eagerly anticipate getting there, regardless of how much you love your family on Earth.

The next time I find myself at death's door, I know I won't be afraid to leave my family and my earthly home. I know my children and my husband have the promise of meeting at the "East Gate." Thank you, Lord.

**Warren, Kasey, Lindsey, Allison,
Nate, Kyle, Wyatt**

CHAPTER NINE

Recovery

Coming home from the hospital was terrifying. I would be alone a lot of the time, because the kids would be at school, and Kenny would be at work. The first day I was home alone, I was on the phone with a friend when my whole left-side began to go numb. She called the church, who called the volunteer fire department and the next thing I knew, my friends were waiting with me for an ambulance. I thought, now, God, really?

It turned out I was allergic to Dilantin, the medicine I had been prescribed to ward off any seizures. They weaned me off of it and put me on Depakote for the next six months.

For weeks, if I took a bath, I would pull the plug as soon as I got in, just in case I had a seizure while I was in the bathtub. I would holler at any one of my kids for ridiculous things. I would have them come find me, to tell them something, or ask them something. What I was really doing was making sure they knew where I was and what I was doing.

At night, I couldn't sleep on the left side of the bed and still don't to this day. I would wake up in the middle of the night in a cold sweat with my heart pounding. I cried a lot for no apparent reason. I felt the worse guilt for being alive when I'd hear of someone's passing. It only worsened when someone I knew would pass away. In my mind, I wasn't good enough to receive the miracle I had. I felt that there were others more deserving, nicer, more important. I slept most of the days, only having enough energy to stay up about two hours. I thought I would never fully regain my energy.

Gradually, I would stay awake until midday. I began baking cupcakes for everyone I knew. It began to be my way of saying I'm sorry. You see I had grown a terrible temper before the rupture. I was so grateful for being alive that I tried to right every wrong I'd done. I did it by baking cupcakes and delivering them with a hug and an apology for the way I had treated them in the past. Poor Kyle, I couldn't drive for six months, so he was my chaperone, and I became his driver's education instructor.

I slept on the couch a lot during my recovery. I couldn't, for one, make myself lie in my bed yet, and two, there was a rack of deer antlers that hung above our bed, and that was scary as well. Once your skull has been taken off and glued back on, you don't take any chances with things that could possibly hit you in the head.

About three weeks into recovery, I woke to a voice I believe to be God's, saying, "Write it down". It was so clear a voice and so commanding and so obvious to me what it was about, I just did it. Through many tears that early morning, I wrote down the "East Gate Story." It was so simply written yet full of rich emotion. I immediately felt it was anointed, and I knew I would share this story, but I had no idea how.

Christmas was just around the corner. Material things meant absolutely nothing that year. I did, however, write thank-you notes and Christmas cards and included a copy my simple story inside. In the back of my mind, I knew there would be something more or God would not have insisted that I write it down. I knew the "East Gate" story had a deeper purpose, and I would be using it somehow in God's plan.

After recovering for a time, baking unending chocolate cup-cakes and crying everyday about everything, God allowed me to return to my old job, full time, on day fifty-six.

I came away from this rupture with no swelling after just one week, post op. I lost no small motor skills or speech. I didn't lose memory or have any seizures. I was weaned off all seizure medicine and stopped taking pain medicine within a week of arriving home from surgery. To date, I am not epileptic, nor do I suffer from headaches.

What I came away with was a praise on my lips for Jesus Christ being the one way to Heaven, and a desire to spend the rest of my days telling others about this miracle I received. To remind others, no matter who we are, where we've been, or what the world tells us will happen next to us, God is still performing miracles for everyday people like us. He can reach us anywhere we are, no matter how far away He may seem.

I'm regretful to say when I moved to Minco, Oklahoma, or as we call it, Minco, America, I did so with great hesitation. Minco had been the rival town of my old high school in Union City. It had always been the place that if you ran from the cops, they couldn't go past the Minco Bridge...at least that's what the teenage hooligans assumed back in the eighties. However, when I became sick, Minco residents did not hesitate to provide support to me and my family. They provided numerous meals for my family. During my recovery, someone would invariably honk at the gate, and I'd send one of the kids out. They would return with a ham or turkey, a sack of potatoes or a bag of oranges, even fish oil (which my neighbor, who I was always a little afraid of, said when people used to be sick, the Bible said to feed them fish. Ha ha!) There wasn't one need that wasn't filled through my church family and MY home-town. I've never seen such a supportive and compassionate town. Now I know firsthand what it feels like to be part of a community.

The first day back at work, I had a dozen people watching me. A bed was set up in an empty exam room, and I was instructed to use it any time I felt tired or overwhelmed. I had good people around me who loved me and would challenge me to do better, but oh, what an emotional wreck I was.

The first week back to work was draining. The physician I was working for, Dr. Fraisure, told me I would be tired for a while. The information in my brain was still there, but now there was a titanium clip that was right in the middle of the road map. My brain had to remap how it would retrieve the information I had stored. Once the route was established, it would become easier and easier. I would be totally exhausted by the end of those days.

I was talking to God daily. I began to ask Him to work in my life and direct me as to what I was to do. Why had He let me live? I was told it would take one hundred days to be one hundred percent again. I anxiously waited for that one hundredth day, and once I had reached it, I felt it was a huge milestone for me.

An acquaintance of mine, Deana, was on my heart during my recovery period. She had been battling cancer and sent her family to see me at the hospital to bring me some 'do rags' for my hair. It struck me odd that someone I barely knew would take time from her own precious time to think of me.

Our children had graduated together from high school and had a graduation party together. A trip to Sam's Wholesale Club was the only time I spent with her physically. I was totally amazed by her. She was celebrating that her cancer had spread to her clavicle instead of an organ. That meant she could live longer, hopefully allowing her to see her youngest child graduate from high school. My youngest is the same age as hers. That could've been me.

There was a wonderful kindness in Deana. She was funny, and she made me feel like I had known her my whole life. For her to send me prayers during my recovery just sealed the deal for me; she was my sister in Christ. Before I went back to work, I was driven to Walmart to do a little shopping. Inside I saw my friend Shelly Vickrey who said, "Deana is outside in the car. You should go say hi to her, she would love to see you." I did. I found her a few cars down from where my car was parked, and I tapped on the window. She sat in the car wrapped in a pink fuzzy blanket, and her eyes sparkled when she saw me. I leaned in, and she wrapped that big old blanket around both of us and hugged me like my dad used to, long and intentional, letting me feel her love.

I noticed she didn't have any hair. Mine was beginning to grow back in already. She was kind of gray in color. My skin was tinted pink against that blanket. She had been fighting cancer for about eight years; I had only fought about eight weeks. My first round of survivor guilt set in.

In the days that followed I began to ponder the "East Gate Story." What was I supposed to do with it? Deana, who was not progressing very well, called and wanted to talk to me about an opportunity she had and a decision she needed to make about going to Tulsa for a last chance treatment. She was exhausted and told me it was hard for others to understand that just being alive was taking everything she had. We talked about how Heaven would be our final resting place, and that East Gate was where we would meet if anything happened. I began to think about ways I could help Deana and her family financially. I knew that after eight years her medical bills must be horrific. My much shorter stay certainly was. I was trying to find a way to help her in the long term.

A t-shirt crossed my mind, an East Gate t-shirt. Days turned into weeks, and weeks turned into months as I procrastinated. I wasted a lot of time as I wasn't exactly sure how to proceed. Occasionally we spoke on the phone, and I would mention an idea to help raise money for her, but it was just talk. Much later Deana's husband Cleo let me know if I wanted to see her, I should stop by. I didn't... she died.

I mourned for several weeks for my special friend. One evening I took my youngest, Lindsey, to a street dance and happened to see Deana's husband. I asked if I could tell him about the story I had written down and explained to him what my plan was for Deana. I felt I owed him an apology for dragging my feet in following through with a fund raiser for Deana. He said, "Do it anyway, for other cancer patients." Just like that, I knew what I was supposed to do. I would make sure cancer patients would get any proceeds from the sale of East Gate t-shirts. I needed a way to distribute those funds and most importantly, figure out how to let people know the one way to Heaven. My Jesus needed to be glorified above all else.

CHAPTER TEN

God Moving

One day my boss Denise Roper called me while I was out of state. She asked if I would consider moving over to the hospital to work for Dr. Stephanie Taylor and Dr. Brady Hagood. I immediately agreed to make the move. Denise suggested I not rush and take my time in making my decision. I told her that she might not understand, but I had been asking God for direction in my life. I stated I had been anticipating His response. When the offer to accept a new position was made, I immediately felt He was opening a door.

Within two weeks, I went to work for the Integris General Surgeons. That poor group received a recovering, guilt-ridden mess. I would spend the next five years with them until they left Integris. It was an incredible season of healing for more than just me, a season of special friendships, and the season East Gate would get off the ground. I shared the East Gate story with the doctors and "the girls." They were a gift sent straight from Heaven, and I've always regarded them in that way.

I had procrastinated to start a foundation and create the t-shirts that I had thought about for so long. The t-shirt would have East Gate printed on the front with a gate and Rev.21:21 on the back. I would give my testimony of the miracle I had received and have the East Gate shirts on hand for purchase. These shirts would be used as a witnessing tool. If someone wore the shirt or if families were wearing the shirt and someone might ask, "What is East Gate?" this would allow for an opportunity to speak with others about the one way to get to Heaven. "It's a family meeting place in Heaven. Do you have one? Do you know the one way to get there?" After all, isn't that what we're supposed to do, tell others about Christ?

The girls in the office would regularly ask me when I was going to start the foundation. When was I going to write the next chapter to my East Gate story? I was by no means a writer (or so I thought at the time), and there were so many things keeping me distracted (healing, family, my new job). I just couldn't stay focused.

One day when I arrived at work, there was an envelope for me with three hundred dollars in it. David Taylor, Dr. Taylor's husband, had done some carpentry work, and in the envelope were his earnings from that job. Dr. Taylor and David had read the East Gate Story many times, trying to decide how they could help me. I was insistent that I should start it, but I just knew someone else should run it. David wanted me to use the money to incorporate and develop the t-shirt and start East Gate. That was just the push I needed to motivate me. I needed someone to believe in my vision, and this loving Christian couple confirmed I was heading in the right direction.

In January 2011, I incorporated East Gate Foundation as a non-profit organization with the primary purpose being to point to Jesus as being the "One way to Heaven." Proceeds from the sale of our t-shirts would go to anyone with serious illness to help defray the costs of things such as prescriptions, food, or gasoline. I chose to help those with any serious illnesses instead of focusing on one health crisis. I felt one day I might have to answer to God as to why I didn't help someone based on which crisis they faced. Six months later, I received my letter from the Internal Revenue Service stating

East Gate Foundation would be a 501C3 non-profit public charity. God is good!

The t-shirt that was designed was in a cream color with brick red lettering. It simply had East Gate printed on the front with a gate and Rev: 21:21 on the back.

ORIGINAL EAST GATE SHIRTS

Now, I thought, where can I share this story?

CHAPTER ELEVEN

Places to Share

M y pastor, Wayne Childers, thought a foundation that could help with travel to chemo would be something the church could get behind. He invited me to come share one Sunday morning. I remember asking Lindsey what she thought I should share with the church, and she responded by telling me I should share the words that God had told me to write down, my East Gate Story. This would be the first time I spoke in front of a large group of people. I was so nervous that I hung on every word the pastor spoke that Sunday, anticipating him calling me to the front of the church. I anxiously sat through the whole service, and before I knew it, the service was over.

Oh, I must have held my breath the entire time. I thought Brother Wayne had forgotten me. He told me later that he felt the Holy Spirit telling him not to have me speak that morning. That evening I came back to services to share my story. I must have cried through my whole testimony. The experience was so fresh and heartfelt that most of the congregation was teary-eyed as well.

One evening, I was at a small women's study group. Deana's friend Shelly was there and mentioned she had heard my testimony and wanted to know how she might become a part of the East

Gate Foundation. She wanted to help in any way she could. I told her I needed someone to keep an accounting of any money raised by the foundation. She agreed to be the treasurer. She remains an important part of this journey.

It was exhilarating to watch God work. My church congregation provided me with the first order for the East Gate t-shirts. The proceeds from that order raised enough money to buy ten $100 gift cards. After Lindsey and I went to Walmart to purchase the cards, I asked her to pray over them with me. Each East Gate card contains a simple scripture from Matthew 11:28. "Come to me, all you who are weary and heavy burdened, and I will give you rest," the story of East Gate, and a gift card worth $100. I kept those gift cards in a lock box in my office at the hospital. The nurses would hand them out when they saw a patient in financial need.

The very first card went to a man by the name of Terry. He had been coming in for weeks with an abdominal wound that wouldn't heal, and his insurance would no longer cover additional treatment. I had already left for the day when Ashley, Dr. Taylor's medical assistant, received a phone call from Terry. He was in the parking lot, and he was crying. He said he had come to his last appointment with no gas in his truck. His wife had left him. He didn't know what he was going to do. Ashley presented Terry with an East Gate card, and when he read the enclosed story, he immediately reached out to his brother, a pastor, who he had not spoken to in several years. He read the East Gate story to his brother, and they talked for quite some time. When they finally hung up, Terry drove to Walmart and was able to buy gas and groceries. He felt like, for the first time in ages, there was hope.

I thought, thank you, Lord! Do it again! A perfect example of how the East Gate cards work is one I share a lot. I learned that a friend's mother was dying of lung cancer. Mitzy, my friend, was planning to take three months from work to be with her. I rarely pass out the East Gate cards; it is usually done through a church or physician. This time I gave one to her, in hopes it would provide some assistance to her with something. Three months later when she came back to work, she shared with me how God was using those East Gate cards.

Misty told me that three days before her momma died, she and her siblings were all together. She told her brother and sisters that she had a story she wanted to share with them. She went on to read the East Gate story to them, and when she finished, she asked her momma if she thought she would like to "pick a gate" with her children. Her mother loved the idea and chose to meet at the South Gate. When questioned as to why she chose the South Gate, she reminded the family of when she taught them to drive. When they were on the interstate, she would always remind them to take the South exit. South would always lead them home. She felt this would be the perfect gate to pick, easy to remember. Mitzy said they were all excited to have a meeting place with their mom, but one of the brothers didn't understand the "one way" to that meeting place. The sisters explained that only through Christ are we able to reach the chosen gate. The brother was led to Christ, right there in the room. Mitzy's mother passed away three days later with a smile on her face. She died knowing that one day she would be reunited with her family.

This is exactly what I envisioned happening with the East Gate cards, and I have personally witnessed it happen many, many times. Thank you, Lord, for paying the price for us. Thank you for being the one way to get to Heaven and preparing a place for all of us who believe in your promise of life everlasting.

CHAPTER TWELVE

Prison Ministry

S hortly after the founding of East Gate, I took a day off from work. I decided I would go to different places to try gaining new opportunities to share my story. I stopped by Ratterman's Insurance in Minco and shared with them what my plans were. That stop led to a phone call and a stop in Union City with Loretta and Roger Norvell. Roger fell in love with the idea of sharing East Gate and told me that he would speak with a pastor who worked in men's prison ministry. I made several stops that day, sharing my near-death story with anyone who would take the time to listen. Each time I told my story, I was overcome with emotion, knowing I had been near death, and had it not been for the grace of God, I would not be alive. By the time I got home that evening, my eyes were red and swollen.

It wasn't long after that when I received a phone call from Mike Rutter, a pastor from Mustang. He invited me to come share my story with about forty men from the Union City Prison at "The Bridge" a church in Mustang. That would be my second opportunity to share my testimony with a group of people. Although I was "scared to death," I trusted the Lord with all my heart, and I was willing to go anywhere as directed by Him. I couldn't dream what to expect. I had no idea of what words would come out of my mouth. I had no outline or notes to speak from. The way I saw it, no one would want to hear what I had to say anyway. They might, however, be interested in what the Holy Spirit would say through me. The first few times I spoke, I felt as though I was being tested. Eventually speaking became second nature, and I was able to relax and embrace all the incredible ways God provided new venues for East Gate.

After I spoke to the inmates, one of the men, a large man in overalls, came to me and said, "You're going to have to learn not to cry around us." Then he handed me a tissue and took one to wipe his own eyes.

**Wednesday night Prison Ministry at the Bridge,
(Volunteer-Sam Dunn praying)**

Each time I spoke, I became more confident that the Holy Spirit would show up and speak through me. I became addicted to seeing God work through the lives of these men. I continue to work with this ministry through the Bridge Mustang Church. I've seen the Lord work powerfully there under Pastor Mike Rutter and with the help of many, many volunteers.

It seems if I don't put God in a box, I see His hand move through East Gate, and He opens doors. His power is greater than any I could ever imagine. The passion I have for speaking to inmates through the prisons, county jails and halfway houses, proves that He is using East Gate to reach people. He opens doors in many different churches of different denominations, as if to say, "Don't limit me."

Some of my most treasured memories have been through kindnesses I have been shown when I was the one who was to minister, yet I was the one more blessed when I left.

I watched a little boy sitting with his mom and dad one evening as I spoke. His mother was trying to keep the little boy quiet, but he was fidgeting with a bag of M&Ms. The more he ate, the more he fidgeted. When his dad would tell him to put the M&Ms away, the young boy would wait a minute or two and get them back out. He did finally settle down and listen to Mike preach.

I had taken a crockpot of sloppy joes to the prison that night, and there was some left over. This was odd, because the men NEVER left anything.... Maybe they didn't care for my cooking that night. Anyway, as we were all leaving, I asked that little boy's mother if she would like to take the remaining food home with her. She could return the crockpot later. She was delighted to accept the offer. As I got to my car, they were walking by, and I called the little boy over and handed him the leftover buns and the remaining bag of corn chips. He flashed the biggest smile. I opened my car door, and I heard him cry, "Wait!" I stopped and waited while he dug in his pocket and unwrapped the last of his peanut M&Ms. I got his last four. That was undoubtedly the best trade ever.

Another act of kindness that touched my heart was from an inmate. After hearing my testimony, he returned to his cell and collected an offering for East Gate. The following week he handed me a paper bag full of change. I feel richly blessed and at home among broken, cracked people such as myself.

Sometimes we witness difficult situations. Once when I spoke at the Canadian County Jail, the pastor told me of a woman there who was demon possessed. She had been chewing off the tips of her own fingers. When I spoke to the women inmates, they all sat quietly with tears streaming down their faces. I believe it was because they had seen evil. Now they recognized the power of God through miracles, mercy, and love. I also saw women who were tenderhearted the evening I went to Mabel Bassett a medium security long term prison. They were on lockdown because of an attempted hanging.

Sometimes we must witness the bad in the world to remember exactly who holds the light in our world. Maybe this changes our perspective enough to recognize His sovereignty. No other name is as powerful as the name of Jesus. What makes the effort worth doing over and over is when we come together as Christians to help someone in need, and they in turn recognize where the gift really came from.

The following is a letter I received after my 'Facebook' family collectively made Christmas happen for a grandmother who had taken in four grandchildren and then found out her cancer had returned.

"Lori! I cannot express words for what I am feeling right now. I am crying tears of joy and happiness for the first time all year. The Lord heard my cry through blessings that my family and I have not had in a while. I have been in a struggle, and the dear Lord told me to sit still. I did and then one day church family and friends came to my door and gave me many blessings to help ease the pain my heart has been burdened with. God is truly a wonderful God! I knew he had not left my side, but I wondered if I would see a light at the end of the tunnel. You and the friends that came to my aid have really given me a way to survive the storm of life. I know the Lord has a plan for me and I must continue to pray and trust He will send many blessings to help me on my journey. I love you all so much for everything you have done to bless me and my grandchildren. Merry Christmas to you and thank you so much. My tears continue to flow for the joy and happiness I am feeling right now. God is good all the time. All the time God is good. He is my all and all."

When her car was loaded with items for her and her grandchildren, the true need was noticed. This woman was driving a vehicle that shouldn't be on the road. When this need was exposed to friends, again the community pulled together and purchased a more reliable car for her. In a very short time, all the money needed for the vehicle was collected. God had even presented the right car for her needs. It was truly beautiful to see Him work through His people.

They will know us by our love....

Keep God out of the box and see what He can do! Through Him, all things are possible.

There was a time, at the beginning of my involvement with the prison ministry, that I spoke to the inmates one Wednesday evening and mentioned the East Gate bracelets that had also been designed to be used as a witnessing tool along with the East Gate t-shirts. The following week, one of the inmates asked if they might be able to get some of the bracelets at the prison. I told the men that I wasn't allowed to give them anything but paper to take back to their cells. Anything else would be considered contraband. One of the men suggested I just leave some on the table next week and "walk away". There had been a time in my life that I wouldn't have had a problem doing that; however, now that just isn't possible. God has been showing me if I want Him to trust me with the big things, then I must first show Him he can trust me with the small things. I responded to the inmate's suggestion of leaving bracelets on the table. I explained to them how important I felt it was that the

East Gate Ministry be able to continue to share the story of God's promise. The inmates hung their heads as they knew I was right.

For the next several days, that conversation played over and over in my head. God had shown me time and time again not to keep Him in a box. If I let Him out of the box, He can do great and mighty things. Then I thought, if gave every inmate in the prison an East Gate bracelet, it wouldn't be contraband. I spoke to Pastor Mike about the possibility of providing bracelets to the entire prison. He told me he would speak to the Case Manager Supervisor at the Union City Correctional Center, Mrs. Ruth Littlejohn.

The following week, I was invited to speak at the prison and was told I could bring bracelets for everyone. This was the first time I felt God move on my behalf bigger than what I was thinking.

The following year an inmate asked if he could buy an East Gate t-shirt. I had to tell him that I couldn't sell him anything while he was confined. Hmmm…. Again, I was led to ask Pastor Mike to speak to Mrs. Littlejohn regarding the t-shirts. I met with Mrs. Littlejohn on a Monday. I was scared to death to approach administration but was drawn to walk into the building and request a face-to-face with her. She met me and escorted me into a room where the two of us could talk with the Chief as well. They let me share what East Gate was and how it would be a positive thing for the inmates to receive a gift like this. It was decided that I could allow every inmate to have a shirt at the time of their discharge from the correctional center. This was exciting! The money needed for the purchase of inmate t-shirts was raised within a week through donations from the community, surrounding churches, and out-of-state donors. I crammed two hundred fifty t-shirts into two plastic totes and delivered them to the correctional center. That's when Mrs. Littlejohn realized I was really "fired up" about East Gate and asked if I might share my story with her.

Thank you, Lord!

**Mrs. Ruth Littlejohn and I with our first
East Gate shirts that surrounding communities
purchased for the inmates.**

She was touched by the anointed story and was instrumental in setting me up to speak at two halfway houses in Oklahoma City and had been instrumental in allowing God into the prison through this ministry. For the last several years, when I can share at the prison, I take in enough East Gate bracelets and stories to share with everyone. God is amazing! I have stayed faithful in ministering to the men through the Bridge Prison Ministry. I attend services and worship with the men every Wednesday evening, even though I belong to First Baptist, Minco.

Sometimes men will tell me they heard my story at the jail, or someone had a copy of it lying on the end of their bed upon arrival to the center. One woman at Mabel Basset told me her boyfriend had shared the story with her over the phone. I love that God is using them to share East Gate!

It was one evening at the Bridge that another conversation stirred my heart. One of the inmates sat down at my table and began talking about how he was scared to be released from the prison system again. His addiction kept him returning each time he was released. He stated that perhaps more Bible study would help rid him of his addiction once and for all. Another man at the table spoke up and shared that he and his "cellie" had started a Bible study on Tuesdays and extended an invitation for him to join them.

That conversation was priceless! I began wondering what tools they had to use in these studies. Did they each have the same Bible, or did they have access to study guides? Again, I was moved to find a way to ease their desire in becoming closer to God. I again went to Mike and spoke about the possibility of providing Bibles for each of the men at the correctional center. By now Mike had started to get used to me. He replied that it couldn't hurt to ask.

I sat on the idea for a couple of weeks, but anytime I had any "quiet" in my day, my thoughts would drift off to the inmate that desired more Bible study within the confines of the prison walls. I subconsciously heard that "Don't keep me in a box." One evening after work, I drove to a Christian book store and decided I would find the right Bible, and then I would go speak to Ruth Littlejohn.

I feel the enemy was already upset at this idea. The salesperson's first words, upon hearing my plan, were to state that there was no way I would be able to get Bibles into the prison. He stated that they used to donate every year to the inmates, but they had been disallowed to continue doing so. (Well, there is that knot in my stomach again.) I explained that I had been involved with them for several years, and I felt confident that I would be able to get Bibles into the prison. I went on to say that I would need enough Bibles for each inmate and each staff member.

I had noticed a sales sign in the store that was offering ten percent off if you purchased ten Bibles and twenty percent off if you purchased twenty. I inquired about the possibility of an even better deal if I purchased two hundred and sixty Bibles. The sales clerk didn't think that would even remotely be a possibility and proceeded to direct me to the Bibles that retailed for $1.99 suggesting those were probably what I was looking for. I responded by telling him I was wanting to look at study Bibles. He showed me a King James version. I know the word of God is powerful even in a small print, pocket size writing, but I felt I also needed to provide Bibles that would meet the needs of those who might have reading disabilities. I chose a different NIV easier reading version. The clerk commented that I was looking at a much more expensive book than the ones on the lower shelves. I thought for a moment about my choice and decided it should have a Life Application version as well. Up the shelf he went, and now I think he tuned me out and saw me as unrealistic. He retrieved a NIV Life Application Study Bible, regular print from the shelf, but my heart reminded me that some of the men might have poor eyesight and have no eyeglasses. These Bibles needed to be in a large print.

The store clerk reminded me that I didn't even have permission yet to bring the Bibles into the prison. I told him I wanted to purchase one to show people what I was thinking. Finally, the salesclerk, after humoring my many changes in what I wanted, sighed and suggested that perhaps I would want them in the color mauve. I reiterated that the men would surely prefer black, and that because this book should last a lifetime, it should be leather bound as well.

By this time, I felt like he didn't even want to sell me one Bible and certainly had no faith in selling me two hundred and sixty. Then I felt the Holy Spirit rush over me! God wanted these men to have the very best. The VERY best! Well, I bought that Bible for $79.99 and asked the clerk to check on the discount for me. I thanked him for his time and walked out and let out a holler.

(Ha-ha!) Not in anger like I would have in the past, but I screamed in exaltation! I felt God's approval and knew He was smiling at my decision. He did want the best for these men. Thank you, God, for allowing this to happen! THANK YOU!

I made several attempts by phone to reach out to that sales clerk over the next couple of weeks with not one returned call. I decided to call the corporate office and tell them of my need and that I found a similar Bible elsewhere on sale for $46.99 and asked if they might match that price. They immediately responded that it would be their pleasure to match that sale price. They even agreed to allow me some time to raise the funds to make a purchase; and regardless of how long it took, they would still honor the sale price of $46.99.

You know, God is our avenger. He sees everything. The next day, I got that return phone call from the salesclerk. He said he had gone to his superiors on this matter, and he was unable to get me any discount greater than the twenty percent discount that we had initially discussed. I told him that I appreciated his return call and his offer, but I had already spoken with the corporate office and secured a price of $46.99 for each Bible purchased. The clerk wasn't a "happy camper."

The following day I met again with Mrs. Littlejohn. I showed the beautiful Bible I had purchased and told her of my desire to purchase Bibles for every inmate and staff member at the prison. I asked if I were to raise the funds to purchase the Bibles, might she allow me to bring them into the center. Without hesitation, Mrs. Littlejohn gave me her approval although she said it would have to go up the ladder. She did make it known that there might possibly be inmates who wouldn't want to accept one. I told her I felt like, once those inmates realized that this was an expensive gift being offered, they would come back and take one. If nothing else, they could give it away to a family member or sell it. I was convinced that if that Bible sat in their cell for the remainder of their incarceration, they would open it. That's all that needed to happen for there to be a great harvest.

It was then I realized Ruth and I were working on the same team. I have never met anyone quite like her. She is a force to be reckoned with. There have been times I've overheard men say they are fearful of her. I think to myself, good, as I am certain she has a role to play inside the prison, and she can't afford to appear "soft." One thing for sure is I'm certain God is using her at that prison. I thank Him for her.

Once I received Mrs. Littlejohn's approval for the distribution of Bibles, I began to work on raising the monies needed to purchase them. I posted on Facebook my need for help in this venture. You know, in a little over three weeks, East Gate raised over twelve thousand dollars. God is capable of amazing things when His followers pull together.

I met many obstacles receiving all the Bibles. One box was missing; four Bibles were missing; arguing broke out in our family; there was trouble at work. You name it, the enemy was in it. One Sunday a dozen men at First Baptist Church of Minco carried box after box to the altars. It was beautiful to see them stacked high and obviously my church needed to pray over these Bibles and the families they would go to.

The day finally came to deliver them. I was so excited! I checked the tires on the truck and made sure there was plenty of gas. I left early even though the prison was only five miles from home. When I arrived with the Bibles, I learned they were on a lockdown because a fight had broken out in the facility. All I could do was smile because God was there with His Holy Word and nothing would stop Him.

I chose not to have any cameras at the Union City Correctional Center because I didn't want to parade inmates in front of them. This was to be a very personal introduction to God for some of them.

Before the first Bible was handed out, the Lieutenant allowed me to speak briefly. My words were these:

"I want you to know these Bibles were purchased by many, many people in your community, the surrounding communities, and even from people across the states. God moved each of them to purchase these gifts as lifetime tools for you because He loves you. He is the God of another chance, and He finds each of you to be valuable. Anything you will ever need is in the box you are about to receive. This book will give you the knowledge to restore your life, your family relationships, and your relationship with Him. It is the living, breathing word of God. There is nowhere in your life that you can ever get that He cannot reach you and change your circumstance. He loves you."

When the time finally came to distribute the Bibles, the inmates were released pod by pod and made a single line through the cafeteria. Two of the inmates opened all the boxes while others passed out the Bibles as the inmates passed through the line. The Lieutenant checked each one off the roster as they each showed their ID badge. I am blessed every day by the path God leads me down with East Gate. As I looked every inmate in the eyes, shook their hand, and whispered "God loves you," I felt His overwhelming presence. Some men were very serious as they came through the line, some were tearful, and some had huge smiles on their faces. Everyone was appreciative. I don't believe I'm over speaking by saying each one of us involved couldn't help but know that at that moment we were witnessing the power of God's work through the distribution of His word. It was the most powerful display of love I have ever seen, in human form anyway. I thank God for my friends and pray each one felt the power of the work He did through them.

The community and churches continue to purchase this special Bible throughout the year averaging about thirty a month. As I type this chapter, they continue to issue every inmate a Bible as they are checked in.

Many people told me that there would be some who wouldn't want the Bible or that some wouldn't take care of it. I asked the staff to try to talk each inmate into taking one and to remind them that it is a valuable gift. Even if they planned to sell it when they got out, that Bible would be ever-present in their cell with them. Why would strangers be so generous in gifting such a beautiful book to so many? Don't you think that at some point curiosity would get the best of them, and they would pick it up, open, and at least look at it? All one needs to do is open that box, and I believe the Holy Spirit will take over from there. God does work in mysterious ways, and His power is great.

Six months after the first Bibles were given out Littlejohn told me by an email the atmosphere in the prison was different. Just because you don't hear about this stuff on the news doesn't mean it's not happening. God still reigns on high!

One evening another inmate named Chuck told me he was working with his cellmate on a sketch for East Gate Foundation. He said they wanted to thank us for the Bibles that continued to come into the facility. I thought that was great.

The next week he came to prison ministry with the picture. He said a few had gathered in his cell giving his cellmate, Sketch, their ideas. One thought the gate was too big because they remembered something about a gate being narrow. Another thought there needed to be stairs but not leading straight to the gate, rather winding because it was a long journey leading them in lots of different ways. They wanted the lettering a certain way.

Finally, their picture was finished! I was so touched. The more I thought about the conversations that were happening inside of the prison, the more I wanted to share with all of the inmates. Shortly after, I had a release signed for the artwork, had a few samples printed by Hineymoon, and soon after received permission from the prison to let each inmate have their own shirt. The community and churches sponsored shirts for each inmate and staff, and we used the money to purchase more Bibles. I love when God does this.

He wasn't finished there. A few weeks ago, an inmate asked me why I chose Sketch's artwork to go on the shirt. He said there were many artists who were much better. I could have chosen one of them. I told him it really didn't have anything to do with the drawing itself. It was the heart behind the gift I wanted to share.

That conversation led to Ruth Littlejohn and me getting together and asking inmates if they would like to draw for East Gate and the best drawings would be put in a calendar. This project is actually just being finished. Calendars will be sold to pay for another round of Bibles. Did I say I love when He does this?

**This is Chuck and Sketch's thank you for the
UCCC study Bibles. Every inmate received
a shirt with this drawing on it.**

CHAPTER THIRTEEN

God Speaking

⌀

After telling my story for three years and wondering if God was going to continue to work through East Gate, I went through a period of disbelief. Was anyone hearing the intended message of East Gate?

Surely there had been wonderful times of sharing the story of East Gate with large groups, intimate groups and one-on-one with individuals, but eventually I felt I was only reaching the same individuals. I needed to share with new people; I needed a new forum. In fact, my accountability partner Lisa Kirkegard even felt as though she could mouth the same phrases I would say when I spoke of East Gate. I only had one story to tell, and surely my current audience would tire of hearing it.

It wasn't long before the pastor of the prison ministry I volunteered with asked me to share my story with a new group of inmates. He would ask two or three times a year or as God guided him to. I have always said yes to any and all requests to speak. In fact, I would say I live to share my Savior through my own experiences. I agreed to speak that Wednesday evening, but in my mind that would be the last time for a while. I wasn't going to burn people out listening to me repeat and repeat my story.

That Wednesday, I struggled through tears sharing my story. I looked into the eyes of strangers and felt connected to each one of them on some level. When I had shared for twenty to thirty minutes, I told of how it would be three years in October that the aneurysm had ruptured and how good God had been to me.

Through my entire testimony there is usually at least one person who starts out by not making eye contact with me, then slowly starts to fidget, and eventually looks at me. That is usually the one who God reaches on a very personal level. That Wednesday night, a very large man sat directly in front of me, and I felt he was glaring at me. When I finished speaking, he stood up, probably six foot four inches or so, and walked straight up to me, bent down to my ear; and I remember thinking I was about to be hurt. He whispered in my ear that his son died from a ruptured brain aneurysm three years ago in October. He said he had been struggling with this and couldn't wait to call his wife and tell her my story. He believed with all his heart that his son was at the East Gate.

In that moment I felt the Holy Spirit, and all doubt I had been feeling earlier disappeared. "I hear you God. I hear you. I will speak where you tell me to speak, and I will let you put the ones who need to hear in front of me."

I drove home that evening elated! I knew God had personally spoken to me, and it was thrilling to get a clear answer. I held on to that feeling for days, but as the week went on, I felt the enemy was whispering in my ear. Surely this had been nothing more than a coincidence. Lots of things happened three years ago in October. There are lots of families who lose loved ones to aneurysms. By the following Wednesday, I had decided not to share my story for a while. I decided to give people a break from hearing my East Gate Story.

On the way to the prison ministry, I was telling Lisa about the scare I had with the inmate last week, and how it turned out. He wasn't angry with me like I thought; he was hurting and trying to share his pain and his story with me.

As we arrived at prison ministry, across the room I saw the inmate I had spoken with earlier. I headed straight to him and shook his hand. I told him I had been thinking all week about what he had shared. I apologized that I hadn't even asked his son's name. He responded that his son's name was Mathias. I had to catch my breath. The only ones in that room who knew my maiden name were God and Lisa and me. My maiden name was, in fact, Mathias. As Lisa elbowed me, tears welled up in my eyes. I felt certain God was speaking to me personally. "Lori, you just speak when I tell you, and I will put in front of you those who need to hear your story." "I will, Lord, I will." Knowing God is talking directly to you is such a motivator. I always know when He's telling me to do something because He speaks in a very personal way, usually only I know, like Mathias. Afterward the inmate introduced us to the woman standing with him.

He said, "I'd like you to meet my wife. Her name is Lisa."

I smiled and nudged my friend...

Lindsey, my youngest, and I have played this game called, "Surprise Me!" for many years. The goal is simply to ask Him to work and then watch for God's hand in your life each day. When you see God's work, it's your surprise for the day. Most of the time only you will recognize Him. For me, it would be deer alongside the road or something like a hawk circling overhead, and I would think, "That's my surprise!" One day, Lindsey and I drove to see her older sister's equestrian drill team out in a very rural area in Oklahoma. While we were talking, she mentioned that she hadn't gotten a surprise that day. I asked, "Have you been watching?" We can see God work in our life everyday if we pay close attention. She spoke with disappointment in her voice that she hadn't received her surprise.

Right in the middle of nowhere, in the middle of the night, we suddenly drove up on a huge, brightly lit billboard. It read "JESUS LOVES YOU". Lindsey shrieked, "There's my surprise!"

I believe you can recognize when He's speaking to you. He makes it very personal and sometimes only you know.

A dear friend of mine, Pastor David Treadaway, told me he had a vision of walking through Heaven with Jesus. As he was being shown around, there was a great commotion from a crowd gathering. David asked what was going on. Jesus pointed and said it was those East Gate people. (Ha, ha! I really hope this to be so.)

I had a sweet friend tell me she had given a slumber birthday party for her daughter. They were trying to figure out a way to incorporate Jesus into her party since many of her daughter's friends and their mothers may not know Jesus. She ran off a dozen copies of the East Gate Story and read it out loud to the families. They were given a copy of the story and then instructed them to go anywhere in the house, the closet, the basement, living room; no place was off limits. They were to read the story together in private and pick a gate.

I thought this was so precious. It was then I realized the Lord was doing something with the East Gate story behind the scenes that I couldn't have possibly ever known about. My hope is that generations from now, someone will find the story folded up in a family Bible, and it will be shared with their families. This side of Heaven, I will never know the ripple effect that will happen over the years, but I believe He is doing a mighty work.

East Gate provided Minco Bulldog shirts to the boys' and girls' basketball teams one year in memory of a beloved teacher, Sara Wittrock, who passed away with cancer. The boys' and girls' basketball coaches read the East Gate story to the kids. I remember Lindsey coming home and telling me the boys' basketball coach pulled her aside to give her condolences on the death of her mother. He couldn't believe that I survived such an ordeal. Lindsey assured him that I was indeed alive and well, and every day I reminded Lindsey to do the dishes. Ha, ha! What a wonderful feeling it was to be alive and to be able to 'get on' that beautiful daughter of mine about her chores. God is so good!

Later that evening, Lindsey shared with me her version of what we went through during the time of my hospitalization. She knows that although we are still just that average family, we have a miracle to recall and the realization that God is still performing miracles today for people just like us. Once when Lindsey was at summer camp, she was asked what her worst memory was. She replied that my health scare was her worst. When she was asked what her best memory was, she replied I was her best.

Thank you, Lord, for my trial.

**Grandbabies Wyatt, Nate
and Presley**

Another time I was amazed by God's ability was when I changed jobs. I had been contacted by the Chief of Nursing at the hospital, Teresa Gray. She wanted to know if I would be interested in transferring to the surgery department full time. I would be coming to help make rounds on the patients and their families to make sure they were comfortable and provide anything they might need. I would help in the department however I could. I would take vitals, clean rooms, schedule surgeries, help with surgery charges and a list of other random chores. I had no idea where God would lead me once I left the surgeons' office, but I trusted His direction.

The first weeks I worked in my newly acquired position, I cried on my way back home in the evenings. It felt so good to be able to serve all day. I couldn't believe I was getting paid to do what I felt to be a blessing. I couldn't help but wonder if this was really where I was supposed to end up. I thought I'd be with the surgeons forever, but now I know it was just meant to be for a season. I questioned whether I "fit" in my new position.

Then I received my answer.

One day I walked past a woman going to surgery on a stretcher. She was looking back at the doorway of her room to the lady who had brought her to the hospital. I overheard her say to the lady to meet her at the East Gate if the surgery didn't go as planned. I thought, "Did I just hear that correctly?" I stopped the woman on the stretcher and asked her what she just said. She repeated exactly what I thought I had heard. When I asked her if she knew me, she replied that she didn't know who I was.

I went on to ask her if she knew the story about East Gate, and she quickly recapped my testimony. I told her that the boy in the story was my son and that I had written that story. She couldn't believe it! I couldn't believe it! She asked me if I'd go back to her room and tell the woman that had brought her the whole story as they had been interrupted. I went back and told my story in its entirety. My boss happened by while I was speaking and gave me a "thumbs-up". This confirmed for me that I was exactly where I was supposed to be.

Two years later, I was nominated and honored with the Stanley Hupfeld Eagle Award from Integris Hospital. It is an award that is given by nomination from the staff and chosen from 10,000 employees. It is for someone who has made a positive impact outside of the workplace. I was honored for the work I do helping those who are ill in the community. A few months later, Channel 4 News paid me a visit at work. They honored me with $400 because of the work in the prison that was taking place. It was Loretta Norvell who turned me in!

I continue to share at every opportunity. I share with hundreds or one, for men, women and children. I share with people from the inner city, the suburbs, of different ethnicities, the deaf, and the Spanish speaking. The Lord has given me a passion to see lives changed and the fire to share with anyone, anywhere. I never get tired of seeing Him work and I am grateful that He uses me in any capacity, until He calls me Home.

I have always been able to hear His voice and recognize when the Holy Spirit is active, but when I had an opportunity to share with a Spanish speaking group, I got a chance to see the Holy Spirit work up close. Let me explain. When I spoke to the group, I had a translator. It was truly a unique experience. I would say one or two sentences and then pause. The translator would repeat my words in Spanish. I have spoken enough times that I can tell the places in my testimony that trigger certain emotions. I can predict a giggle based from past experiences, and I also recognize where people normally get choked up. When I came to the moment where I testify that Kyle said, "I know, Momma, but I remember East Gate." Most people have a reaction. Not this time, not one person moved, changed their expression, or connected with me until the translator spoke repeating my words. It was in that moment, I witnessed the power of the Holy Spirit move those people in a wave, from left to right. It was priceless to see such a reaction.

CHAPTER FOURTEEN

Faith Riders

I'll never forget the Sunday I agreed to ride with the Faith Riders, a Christian motorcycle club. My husband is the motorcycle enthusiast, not me. I'm scared to death of an accident and the possibility of a head injury. Despite my fear and because I love Ken, I decided to accompany him on a ride. Kyle, my son, rode with a friend behind us.

Unfortunately, the rider in front of us had a blowout on the rear tire of his motorcycle. We managed to get everyone pulled over to the side of the road without incident, but we had about a three hour wait before we were able to obtain tow services to a Harley shop to have a new tire put on. Once a new tire was mounted, we decided to end our ride at a stop on Mount Scott, the only "mountain" in Oklahoma.

Once we arrived at the top, we thought our middle-aged group was the only one in the area. It was then we noticed a group of young rappers shooting a video just over the edge of the mountain. We were a bit startled and concerned for our well-being because they appeared to be a gang, mostly men with only a couple of women, all dressed in red. When we finally took time to listen to the lyrics they were reciting, we realized they were referring to

Christ in their lyrics. Much to our surprise one of the young men came to the top of the mountain. He told us the name of their group was Alpha Team. This rap group's purpose was to come together with other Christians to promote Jesus Christ. Then the producer asked us if we would like to appear in the video they were filming. Since the temperature was near a hundred degrees that day, all the women wearing helmets declined the offer (not a good look for our hair). The more I thought about the possibility that God had a hand in putting this offer before us, I asked if they might just include the blue East Gate shirt I was wearing in the video. The producer, without hesitation, agreed. The next thing I know, I'm in between two large men, about twenty-five years younger than me. The entire group was dancing and raising their hands, taking turns singing and praising my sweet Jesus. I was so embarrassed. The worst part was that my husband and my son were standing in front of the large group watching Mom. They were standing, arms crossed, shaking their heads at me. Ugh!

ALPHA TEAM at Mount Scott

The producer began talking with the group I was riding with while I took part in the video. He asked what East Gate was and what it was all about. When I was finished with the video production the producer approached me and began talking about a world label video he was working on. He said it would be free to people to promote Christ as our Savior. He wanted permission to put the East Gate website at the bottom of the credits.

There He goes. My God continually teaches me if I listen and go where He tells me, He will use me. This was one of many lessons He taught me on this subject of going where He leads. Oh, what precious lessons!

Ken and Kyle still can't believe Mom was in a video. You must love God's style.

Later that year, I invited an ex-inmate to speak the Sunday of the East Gate Spaghetti Dinner, and Alpha Team came to sing and rap and got my precious Southern Baptist Church members to raise their hands in worship! I thanked God when the Team members asked permission to show the video on screen. To their dismay and my delight, the projector was broken. Thank you, sweet Jesus! If anyone would like to see the video, it can be found on you tube music: "Can't Stop Me" by AlphaTeam.https: ://youtube/ ZCRm270sLODES Gospel Family.

The nearer I get to finishing this book, the more distractions and whispers try to stop me. I feel the enemy's hatred. Because I long for Christ's approval, I have a huge target on me. I was told to write this, knowing all too well I am not a writer. The Holy Spirit will have to finish this if it is to be completed in two years as God has dictated. Some days the torment mentally pushes me to my very limits, but then the Jesus in me overcomes.

Lord, some days I have doubt planted in me that I am not up to the task at hand. I've been misunderstood most of my life, so I know that writing all these things leaves me very vulnerable. I pray this book makes it to hands of those who need to read it for Your glory. Lord let me live to finish it. I pray my trials be turned into a legacy for my family and friends, to allow them to grow closer to You, and encourage them to pick up where I leave off.

All for Your glory, Lord!

CHAPTER FIFTEEN

God Uses Everyone

ﾃﾞ

One day, I stopped at the Dollar Store on the way home. There was a former drug dealer in town. He was divorced, his children were grown, and he had taken in a cousin who was dying from cancer. His cousin had four children, ranging in age from infancy to teens, each with a different father, none of whom were involved in their child's life. I asked him what he was going to do when the children's mother passed away. He said he was going to try his best to keep them together. He had a court date scheduled to try to obtain custody of them.

East Gate had given him a gift card at Christmas time to help with expenses. Again, I asked him what his needs were, and asked if he could use another East Gate card. He declined my offer and instead felt compelled to do something for East Gate. He wanted to contribute to the car fund set up by East Gate to help that someone who was in dire need. Even after I explained the total $3,000 had been raised for the car East Gate was purchasing for a Grandmother with cancer, my friend still insisted on contributing, stating that money was currently not important in the scope of his circumstance. Having made his feelings known, he pulled out his wallet and gave me three hundred dollars. All I could do was hug my brother in Christ as tears welled-up in my eyes.

Thank you, Lord, for letting me see this man come full circle. When we see your power right before our eyes, how could we deny Your ability to transform people?

Several months ago, I was reminded of a lesson on being bitter. There was a man named Patrick who came to the Prison Ministry at the Bridge. He came forward for us to pray for his daughter Delaney who was three years old and had been diagnosed with leukemia. He said he wanted to prepare his heart for her death, but he also wanted to claim complete healing for her. He was torn. He didn't want to be angry with God if the healing didn't happen.

My heart hurt for Patrick. I've been bitter toward God before. It only hurts worse to not talk to the one who holds the World when it feels like your world is falling apart. The volunteers prayed for him that night and promised to continue to pray for him and his little girl. Patrick was released about two weeks later.

After a few weeks, I stopped Pastor Mike to ask if he would check in on Patrick and see how he was doing. Mike did check in on him and subsequently called me with a need. Patrick and his mother were trying to come up with funds to take a bus from Oklahoma City to Albuquerque and stay at a Super 8 motel for a week to be with Delaney at the cancer center. Delaney had just gone on hospice.

I've seen God work in so many ways that I never can predict what will happen next.

Shortly after I heard of Patrick's circumstance, I received notice that the Minco First Baptist Vacation Bible School had picked two different local non-profits to help that year. They had collected several hundred dollars to be divided between a blanket ministry, Deedah's Covers of Love, and The East Gate Foundation. Those donations provided enough for round-trip bus tickets for Patrick and his mother to go see precious Delaney. They had enough to stay a week at a Super 8.

Isn't that just like God? A little girl and her mother in New Mexico, an inmate without funds to travel to his ailing daughter, and a group of children raising an amazing amount of money allowing that family's needs to be met. All was possible through the compassion and mercy of our loving God. Delaney passed away a couple of weeks later, but Patrick was blessed to have been able to reunite with his little girl before the Lord called her home. This new Christian saw God up close and personal. I love our God!

God's been trying to teach me how priceless we each are to Him. ALL of us are equally important to Him. I've known for a long time that age, mental and physical challenges, financial status, past mistakes, etc., do not limit how God sees us or how He uses us.

Every October, I become withdrawn and moody, to say the least. I dream a lot and feel like a rope is tightening around my neck. Let's just say the enemy has a great deal of time with me, causing me to be anxious and doubt what I do with East Gate.

There are still times my heart is heavy. Survivor's guilt tries to whisper blame for death, replay how the ending might be different if only I had done something different, or if I had done it sooner. The truth is our Lord could raise any one of us up this very moment if He chooses to. It isn't in our hands at all. The one thing we can do is make sure our families know where we will be going and the one way to get there. You never know when He will call you home.

Then I start remembering the miracle that was given to me and the undeserving mercy that was poured out, the passion for people that was given to me. Never forget God can reach you, wherever you are, no matter how hopeless it seems. The trial is what changes you and brings God back to first place in life. Then living can truly begin. I'm so grateful for the second chance I've been given.

Sometimes I need to be shown again and again, repeatedly reminded not to count anyone out. I recently met with an eighty-year-old woman in a nursing home who has fought with mental illness her whole life. She doesn't see well or walk well or breathe well on her own. God thinks she is priceless and is still using her for His glory. The woman I speak of is my mother. God uses every one of His children if we let Him.

**My mom seeing her
grandbaby Wyatt for the first time**

Thank you, Lord, for giving me that priceless woman to be my mother, my encourager, and my teacher. Forgive me when I set limits on people you value. Forgive me when I set limits on You, praying to always see through Your eyes and with Your heart.

My family tries to travel home to Illinois at least once or twice a year. The older Mom gets, the tougher it is to say good-bye. She always whispers when I hug her, "Don't cry for me, Honey. If something happens, you know where I'll be." Oh, I love her.

Don't forget to talk ahead of time!

CHAPTER SIXTEEN

A Financial Healing

B efore the rupture happened, we had planned to build on to our little farmhouse. I'd always wanted a big open living room/ kitchen. I wanted to add on a second level over a garage. We had only been able to replace fourteen windows, some electrical work, and some painting.

The financial weight of having children that were in school, going to go to college, and the heavy burden of thirty medical facilities, and groups sending us bills was overwhelming. Every arteriogram was a new procedure; and, of course, the entire time I was in the hospital, I was totally out of my network. $189,000 was our part of the medical expenses incurred from the aneurysm.

Ken and I had decided during my hospital stay that if we had to take whatever was left of our incomes at the end of the month and divide it by thirty for the rest of our lives to pay off the debt, then that would be what we would do. It was certainly worth any amount of money for the life I gained in return.

This became a state of mind, whatever it takes. I've got to be honest, that Christmas none of us had a single want.

**Tiny kitchen: Warren, Kenny,
Kasey, Lindsey and Bub**

The following year, God revealed why He had put us in that little farm house. We had previously had a beautiful new home in Illinois that was built by my dad, my brothers and my husband. I struggled with living in Oklahoma in a little nine hundred ninety square foot home with a family of five.

The year following my surgery, we were contacted by the Department of Transportation of Oklahoma. They wanted to use part of our land for a new highway project. They needed our barn by two inches and about a foot of our property down one side of the house.

After calling each physician and each medical group that we owed money to and working with them to make a payoff deal, we had just enough money to pay off all the bills. Wow! We never saw that coming. God is truly amazing, and the way He works cannot be predicted or put in a box.

CHAPTER SEVENTEEN

East Gate 5K/10K

One day a friend in my Sunday School class, Joey Fitzgerald, asked me if I had ever considered putting on a 5K for East Gate. If I recall correctly, I said, "Absolutely not!" and then laughed. He told me about some that he had participated in. I told him I would surely think about it.

I was looking through my e-mails about a week later when I came across one about a Director's Workshop for 5K's. Within moments, Joey called me to tell me about a production company called DG Production Company that helped put on 5K events. It just so happened the DG Production Company was putting on the workshop I signed up for.

For me, that coincidence was my signal to do it. I signed up, went to class, took notes, and then did my homework. Over the next few months, I went to several 5K runs and shadowed the directors until I finally felt confident enough to set my own date. The purpose for East Gate's 5K would be different than other 5K's that were put on to raise money. My run would be to raise awareness about the one way to get to Heaven. If the foundation ever became about raising funds, it would be over before it ever started.

East Gate has always been about pointing to Christ. The idea was this: We would reach outside our community and sanction this race as a United States Track and Field (USTAF) certified race. We would shower our runners with so much love and spoil them. We would create an event that people would return to year after year and, hopefully, bring in new people each year. The idea was to use the East Gate t-shirt as a witnessing tool, explain how to use it, give great trophies, free food, and then pull names for some wonderful prizes!

Just imagine, loving on people for an afternoon, treating them so well that they would go home and wonder what East Gate was all about. It would be awesome to promote the tool that would promote the one way to Heaven. East Gate has held five sanctioned 5Ks. Four of the races were held in Minco, Oklahoma, and one in Decatur, Illinois. We added a 10K to the last two events with a family member adding one thousand dollars to the pot to the male and female first-place runners to be divided equally.

East Gate 5k held in Minco, Oklahoma

Every year East Gate has honored or remembered someone who has faced the fight against cancer. The first race was in memory of the dear friend of mine Deana who lost her battle. Her husband leads out the race every year in a vehicle and lets the family ride with him. Deana forever holds that special place and has been the inspiration for me to make East Gate's focus on those who are facing cancer.

My friend Roger Norvell was the person honored at the second East Gate 5K. Roger always gathered prizes for the giveaways at the races, continually supported East Gate, walked in the event and got me involved in every aspect of prison ministry. He developed terminal liver cancer a few years ago. I can't tell you what a great man the world lost when he succumbed to cancer. He truly loved people, not just the easy-to-love people. He loved the hard-to-love ones most. Roger didn't care where you came from or what your current circumstance was, he loved you regardless.

Roger and his wife Loretta came to our home once and asked if he could be a stand-in Grandfather to our youngest, Lindsey. He felt she was an amazing young lady, and he wanted to be there for her should any need arise. He also gifted our family with a beautiful cross that he built. That large cross stands lit in our yard year around. Roger and Loretta have been very supportive of my work in East Gate and always helped anywhere needed.

When the day came to see Roger one last time, Lindsey and I had a difficult time saying good-bye. As we sat quietly holding his hand, he asked if he might pray for us. Regardless of what he was facing, he was concerned for us. He prayed, "Lord, I pray you watch over Lindsey and her family, and if there is a balcony in Heaven, allow me to look over at special times…when Lindsey graduates and gets married and has children. Remind them how much I love them and how good you are taking care of me. In Jesus's name, Amen."

Roger spoke with the inmates from his bed.
Told them he loved them.

Roger died two days later.

Before my friend took his final breath, he requested donations be made to East Gate Foundation in lieu of flowers. I wasn't
sure what to do with such a donation. I thought about putting "In
memory of Roger..." inside each East Gate gift card. Soon it
became apparent exactly what Ol' Roger wanted me to do with
any donations. I still smile at how God worked it all out. Roger had
done so much for the prison ministry that Littlejohn allowed some
of the inmates to attend his funeral. When I arrived at the funeral,
it just felt right to sit with those inmates. Just as I sat down, one of
the pastors came and said, "Roger would have wanted all of you
to sit with the family." We all got up and moved over to the family
side. The inmates sat right behind me.

One of the pastors who was speaking about Roger presented a
challenge to each of us. He asked who would pick up the mantle

now that Roger is gone. Who was going to be the one to love unconditionally as Roger had done? At that moment, the entire two rows of inmates humbly stood up behind me with their heads down. That gesture was indicative of how Roger had influenced those men.

There was a large sum of money donated in Roger's name to the East Gate Foundation. Those monies sat idle until about two weeks later when a pastor from the Fortieth Street Baptist Church called me. He explained that although we had never met, he heard how the foundation has helped those with cancer. He said there was a homeless man that attended his church on occasion. The man he spoke of was named Terry, had liver cancer and walked to chemotherapy treatments. The pastor said that any help East Gate could offer would truly be a blessing for Terry. He went on to tell me that Terry was single, his daughter was not speaking to him, and his son was in prison.

I now knew exactly how to use Roger's donation.

Within a few days, we were able to lease one side of a duplex for him for two months. Additionally, there was enough money left to help with food and power. I posted on Facebook the need of a refrigerator and within minutes someone donated one and another volunteered to pick it up and deliver it. The Baptist Church helped him fill out paperwork for disability, and he was approved and received a check before the third month's rent was due.

Terry's landlord occupied the space in the other half of the house. This landlord took care of his sick grandmother and a niece who was mentally challenged. When I met with him to pay Terry's rent, he told me a little of his history. He said the duplex was in danger of being taken because of unpaid back taxes. He desperately wanted to take care of his family and decided he could watch over a couple more people. When I wrote him the first month's rent check for four hundred seventy-five dollars, I was talking to him and asked if he would mind confiding in me the total amount of his past due taxes. That landlord took the check, smiled and with tears in his eyes said, "Four hundred seventy-five dollars."

Before Terry passed away, he had come to have a family. He had been able to talk to his son a couple of times, and he made amends with his daughter. Most importantly, he reconciled with the Lord.

God is more than we could ever imagine. He is so good. I sure hope Roger was leaning over that balcony.

The third race was to be held honoring a man by the name of Gary who started an online ministry, "Light Ministry." He fought colon cancer while ministering to hundreds of people including me. I didn't want to wait for Gary to be on the list someday. Instead of holding the next race "In Memory Of...," it was decided it would be "In Honor Of...." (My husband has an Aunt Wanda who has said that she wants no flowers at her funeral. She said she wants to receive them while she is alive to enjoy them and the sentiment that comes with them.) Gary received his trophy that read Philippians 3:14, 'I press on toward the goal to win the prize for which God has called me heavenward in Christ Jesus,' and felt the love while he was alive. I feel certain God had a crown waiting at his finish line. He was indeed a special friend.

The fourth East Gate race was in memory of a family member. My nieces Markesha and Marjanai lived in Decatur, Illinois. The girls wanted to know if I would come hold a 5K for their little brother Mark. This young man's death was totally unexpected and happened so quickly. It allegedly resulted from an arm injury he sustained while playing basketball.

That was a difficult race to hold. My family all went above and beyond to gather sponsorships, prizes for the drawings, and handouts for those participating. My niece Dee even gained a radio spot for the race along with billboard advertisement. Mark's sisters were able to tell about this incredible young man and hopefully gain some closure. They have since started the "Lil' Mark Warrior Fund" to award a scholarship in his name each year at the school he would've attended. Mark will never be forgotten. This race was a reminder of the one way to see him again. Through Christ we are promised an everlasting life in His kingdom. Thank you, Lord!

My Decatur, Illinois family

**Lisa Kirkegard, Kim Norman-Scott,
Gary Chester, Brenda Miller, Lynny Baker**

Last October we held our fifth race. We honored the memory of Sara Wittrock. While I was at Lindsey's high school graduation, I heard how one of the teachers had passed away. This teacher left a great impression on all her students. There had been a scholarship fund set up in Sara's honor, and the recipient of the scholarship that year was a young girl by the name of Sydney. Sydney was able to give Sara's husband Troy one thousand dollars from the proceeds of that East Gate 5K whereby ensuring that the scholarship would continue.

God is good.

This year we changed it up a bit. I felt the race was slowing down and now would be a good time to do something different from a sanctioned 5K. We held a night time unsanctioned cancer walk, leaving from the new high school in Minco, Oklahoma, and making a complete 5K square. It was called the East Gate Glow Walk and was so much fun. We carried the cross Roger built me and put a thousand lights on it. It was carried the entire 5k. Let your light shine was our theme! Prizes were given for brightest, most colorful, most original, funniest, and most original. (The honoree actually won this for her glow in the dark dreadlocks.)

East Gate 5k/Glow Walk

There was a celebration/worship service afterward lead by Keith Ingram and special guest Jami Smith. I could hardly wait to honor my dear accountability partner. She has played an important part in East Gate from the very beginning. Lisa Kirkegard has been in twenty-year remission from breast cancer and just found out it has come back.

Lisa started her own ministry last year and calls it "Deedah's Covers of Love." It is a blanket ministry honoring a lifelong friend, Geraldine (Geri) Hines, who lost her battle with cancer. Geri used to help East Gate with dinners and the race when she felt well. Lisa's ministry has reached 36 states, and given over eighteen hundred blankets away, including sending one to Delaney, the little girl from Albuquerque, who succumbed to cancer.

With the help of Geraldine's husband Jerry, and a few friends, we surprised her with 129 blankets draped over the stadium chairs and several made a video telling her how much we loved and cared for her, except for me. I told about how she was my actual partner in crime and nearly got us kicked out of prison ministry. Ha-ha. I've seen God work miracles. I'm praying for one for my dearest friend.

When I reflect on the race each year, I wonder, was He pleased? Did we point toward Him? With all the sponsorship and volunteers who give without gain every year, I know He is.

CHAPTER EIGHTEEN

Dirty Old Rags

I have tried to be as transparent as possible while writing this book. Anyone who thinks highly of me, please don't! I can only boast of my weaknesses as they are many. Anything good that I have ever done was only possible through the power of Christ working in me. You need to know that I've learned a valuable lesson and now try not to show the ugliness I once did...especially toward car salesmen.

Immediately after the surgery, my poor Sonata started getting the life beat out of it. I had raised my deductible and a lot of other things to help pay down medical bills, so the first two hailstorms the car had been in, I didn't have it fixed. From there it just got worse.

One of the kids drove it to school and someone backed into the driver's side back door. We were paid cash not to turn it into their insurance company. Just weeks after that, Ken and I were on the interstate where a wreck occurred. We were rear ended when the car behind us didn't see we were stopping.

When Lindsey and I drove to Guymon, Oklahoma, to visit Kasey at college one winter, the passenger window was rolled down and never came back up. My son-in-law Warren rigged it for us with duct tape allowing us to get home. As it neared the end of the car loan, the visors, passenger handles, even the rearview mirror had fallen off.

Finally, Lindsey was shooting baskets outside the fence one night. I asked her to lay the basketball hoop down when she came in; but with her selective hearing, well, you already know how the car fared when a storm came through Minco that night. When I went to take Lindsey to school the next morning, she gasped and covered her face as we noticed my driver's side mirror was completely gone. I couldn't even react. When we got in the car, she said, "Mom, are you okay? Are you going to yell or something?" All I could do was laugh. That car was the last thing I found any value in.

Every five years my husband and I have alternated purchasing a new vehicle. We both drive about an hour round trip to work and put quite a few miles on our vehicles. This was his particular year to trade in his truck; but since he had been allowed to bring home his squad car at the end of his shift for the last five years, and mine had taken a beating, he thought I should get the new car. I have never liked the "dance" of looking for, driving, or purchasing a new car. In fact, it makes me sick to think about car shopping. Because I do not like the process of new-car buying, I agreed with the stipulation that Ken pick out the car. Without hesitation he went to different dealerships sending me pictures of different vehicles, and finally found the one he thought we needed. It was a perfect mid-sized car, but there was one problem I would have to deal with. I would have to go to the dealership to sign paperwork, as well as Kenny. Well, Blah! This is where my attitude began to surface. I was assured it would only take a minimum amount of time. In and out. All I had to do was meet him over at the Norman dealership about six-thirty p.m. and sign the necessary papers.

I dreaded the drive over to Norman. I already felt the ugliness welling up in me. I thought to myself, I'm going to go in, sign and go back out to wait for Ken. Why do I despise this so very much?

Was it because the last dealership I went to they basically asked me to leave? Ugh! I hated the process.

I met Ken at the dealership ignoring all the staff, trying to be nice, and just get through this. I immediately assume the salesman is the enemy; He just had that "look". Just as we sat down to finish the paperwork Ken's pager went off. He was on call that evening and had to leave. He signed his part of the contract and said, "Honey, just sign your part, and drive the car home. You'll be okay, it won't take long."

I felt certain that they were going to try to take advantage of me since I was there alone. Another salesperson came in and sat down. Now they've teamed up on me. They tried to sell me an extra warranty and what seemed like a dozen other things. Finally, we came to an understanding that I was only signing my name and then leaving. At that point the second salesperson handed me a paper sack and asked me to take out the remaining items in my old car. Just that phrase felt insulting. I had a serious problem with my attitude.

As I began to remove things from the old car, I was aware of the salesman standing outside the car waiting for me. I started packing CD's and emptying pockets in the car, and then I started to remember how I taught Kyle and Lindsey to drive in that car. There were a few spots on the floor where prison ministry food had spilled and left the carpet stained. I realized that not too long ago, I never expected to be around to ever have anything new again. I truly didn't expect to live more than a couple of years, only long enough to tell the story of East Gate. Then I saw the www.east-gatefoundation.com sticker in the back window of the car. A flood of emotions came over me, and I began to cry. In that moment, I heard God speak to me. He said that he didn't just want to heal me physically; He wanted to heal me financially, in my relationships, in every aspect of my life, if I would only let Him.

The salesman handed me my new keys and asked me to please tell him what was wrong. He said he didn't want me to leave feeling badly. I opened my mouth, and everything I was feeling came out! I said I didn't want a new car! I wanted to keep all the memories that were in the old car. I didn't feel I deserved a new car. The family had taken trips in the old car, and my East Gate website was on the rear window. Blah, blah, blah…

That salesman told me he would go get a razor to scrape the website off the back window if that would help. He asked me what was East Gate? He really wanted to know what it meant.

Well, heck! Now I'm starting to like him…just a bit. I began to share the underlying causes of my emotions with him and gave him a very short testimony of what East Gate meant to me. Once my story had been told, he said to me, "Mrs. Rush, I know our business here is complete, and it is closing time for us, but might I ask you a favor? I have a friend inside that really needs to hear your story. Will you come in and share with him?"

Now, I do like him. I'm humbled and I feel the Lord standing with me. I told him, "Yes, I will."

He walks me over to his desk in the middle of the room. Looking around I could tell everyone was getting ready to close. The salesman picked up a microphone and asked all personnel to please come to his desk. A dozen salespeople of all ages and various ethnic backgrounds came to gather around his desk. At this time, he explained to the staff that I had just purchased a car from the dealership and had shared a beautiful story that he felt they needed to hear. He motioned for me to begin speaking.

I shared my testimony of what the Lord had done for me; I watched the faces of strangers begin to connect with my story, and some cried with me, yet others were very sober. I told them that I had come to terms with facing death and recognized that the possibility of me ever purchasing another new vehicle was nil. I didn't feel I deserved anything of value anymore until the Lord spoke to me while I was cleaning out the old car. "I want to heal every aspect of your life."

One of the sales managers asked if he might pray for me before I left. That group of salespeople got in a circle with me, and that sales manager went completely around the circle of men and prayed for each one's family. When he got to me, he prayed, "Lord, thank You for sending Lori today. Thank You for reminding us today of Your love and power. I pray blessings over her and her family; I pray that her new car will continue to help her do prison ministry. I pray You keep her safe and prosper her ministry all the days of her life. In Jesus's name, Amen."

Have you ever felt God tap you on your shoulder? I did! I heard Him say, "I work here, too, Lori." I cried tears of all emotions on the way home that evening. I was so ashamed of myself, but the Lord taught me a lesson about people and myself that I was and am forever grateful for. We are all the same, dirty old rags, if not for the blood of Jesus.

Those men at the dealership got an East Gate t-shirt order together and called me the next day. At my first oil change, I saw men wearing the East Gate bracelets. I had called ahead and asked the manager if I could talk to him about something his men had done for me last time I was there. He said, "Oh, God, did they do something?" Ha! Ha.

When I shared with him and shared my testimony with him, he said, "I always knew I had good men working with me. I just never knew how good." He offered to sponsor our first 5K that year – Bob Moore Nissan/Norman.

God has allowed me to be a witness to the following events East Gate has held over the last eight years: three dinners, six blood drives, five sanctioned US Track and Field 5K/10Ks in two states, held a segment on TBN, and a night time cancer walk. I've been blessed to speak at many banquets, small to large, all ages, a youth revival, a family reunion, for a college basketball team and even various groups at the local school.

The Lord has repeatedly opened doors and given me opportunities to share East Gate with men's and women's prisons, county jail and halfway houses. Through help from the community, the foundation has given almost a thousand leather, Life Application Study Bibles; thousands of copies of printed testimony; thousands of wrist bands and around six hundred East Gate t-shirts to the prisons alone.

East Gate has been blessed to partner with many churches and businesses over the years. First Baptist Church Minco, First Baptist Pocasset, Hazel Dell Baptist Church, Assembly of God Minco, Heaston Community Church, Trinity Church, Main Street Church, Cogar United Methodist, Canaan Baptist, Village Baptist, and Laverty Baptist, to name only a few! All of us together have been able to provide travel expenses, prescriptions and groceries. I've been able to share with such a diverse group of people and given over $100,000 in Walmart gift cards alone. More importantly, numerous lives were changed as they received the Lord as their Savior.

I pray the Lord lets me see the giving of a million dollars to those in crisis for His glory and still be content in my little farmhouse. No one will be able to deny this was all God. Nothing so wonderful could have happened without His hand moving. I am so richly blessed.

When I think of all the beautiful things I've seen and experienced on this journey with East Gate; and I think of all the anonymous donors who have given faithfully, unselfishly, without hesitation to the foundation, my heart swells. If it weren't for all of us imperfect people working together for the Lord, East Gate would fail to thrive. I am forever humbled to have even seen a glimpse of His splendor. Thank you for coming together for strangers to make their lives easier in the face of sickness through transportation, food or medicine. It's Him using you who makes this ministry work. I wish I could repay you for all you do here on Earth, but I am reassured that, on the other side, the fruit of your labors will be seen and acknowledged. I love you, friends. "They will know us by our love."

It is without a doubt the most life-changing journey of which I have been part. The most valuable perspective changed is it's all about people, not things;

It is about dirty old rags made clean.

Addendum: I finished the last section of the book on a Saturday. On Sunday, I went to church, and a realtor pulled me aside and asked if we would be interested in selling our property. She thought she might have a buyer interested. I looked at her funny thinking absolutely not. I had been bitter about this place in the past and I had just gotten over it, and even wrote in my book I wanted to stay in that humble farmhouse. I meant it and told her no.

The next day Kenny called me at work and said, "You're not going to believe this. Mr. Locke asked me if we ever considered selling our home and property? He said he would be interested in buying and could he have an appraisal done and get back with us."

Two days later, Mr. Locke made an offer that was too good to be true. Kenny and I did what a Christian couple would do when they felt God was just blessing them. We checked with oil wells, pipelines, mineral well drilling, etc.... No one had secretly found a fortune on our humble little property. We couldn't help but wonder what God was up to.

Shortly after, we found a house back in the little town where Ken and I both graduated. We bought an almost new beautiful brick home in Union City and sold ours in 30 days. God confirmed the buy, not from using my maiden name of Mathias, but the owner's daughter did ask where we were from. I told her, "Illinois." She asked, "What part of Illinois are you from?" I said, "Decatur, Illinois." She touched my arm and said, "Honey, I'm from Decatur." That sealed the deal for Ken and me.

Picture of new home

So how does that happen? During our real estate purchase process, the Lord spoke to me. I had secretly longed for something more for years. I finally just wanted Him and learned the lesson that it wasn't about people or things like I so proudly boasted I had figured out. It was about Him. The moment I realized I could be anywhere with Him and longed for people to know it was all Him from the beginning, it was as if He said, "Ok, now let's move." I had spent years trying to learn that lesson and finally I did. My devotion that day was, "It's time to turn north, beloved." Deuteronomy 2:2-3

Without Him, we are nothing, going nowhere. We can't even love people without loving Him first. It's all about Him.

**Lori Rush/Founder East Gate Foundation
(with beautiful Momma)**

About the Author

⁊⁊

I continue to enjoy my family and my new home. I'm blessed to be here to see my grandbabies grow up! I love to share what God has done for me. I'll speak wherever He leads. Maybe that could be for your church or group function? Follow me on Facebook and be part of East Gate. I learned a long time ago if you see God working somewhere, go there! It takes every one of us doing our part to spread His word.

Anything else I could tell you about myself really doesn't matter. Eternity does. My perspective has forever been changed. Do I still have a bad day? Yeah. Do I worry about finances? My dishes? Yeah. But at the end of the day, when it is still, I know who holds my future and all is well. What a beautiful Savior.

Talk about eternity on purpose with those you love. Do it now!

www.eastgatefoundation.com

"For it is by believing in your heart that you are made right with God, and it is by openly declaring your faith that you are saved." Romans 10:10

"For God so loved the world that He gave His only begotten son that whosoever believes in Him, shall not perish but have eternal life." John 3:16